Critical Guides to French Texts

104 Etcherelli: Elise ou la vraie vie

Critical Guides to French Texts

EDITED BY ROGER LITTLE, WOLFGANG VAN EMDEN
AND DAVID WILLIAMS

ETCHERELLI

Elise ou la vraie vie

Sara Poole

Lecturer in French,
University of Reading

Grant & Cutler Ltd
1994

ISBN 0 7293 0368 3

I.S.B.N. 84-401-2126-1

DEPÓSITO LEGAL: V. 4.731 - 1994

Printed in Spain by
Artes Gráficas Soler, S. A. - La Olivereta, 28 - 46018 Valencia
for
GRANT & CUTLER LTD
55-57 GREAT MARLBOROUGH STREET, LONDON W1V 2AY

Contents

For my parents

Prefatory Note

Two editions of *Elise ou la vraie vie,* originally published by Denoël in 1967, are available: a French edition in the Gallimard Folio series (1972), and a British edition in the Twentieth Century Texts series (Methuen, 1985; reprinted Routledge, 1989), with an introduction by John Roach. References in the present volume are to *both* texts, and take the form of two page numbers, in parentheses, and separated by an oblique stroke, e.g.: (p. 9/55). The first number refers to the Folio edition; the second, to the Twentieth Century Texts edition.

References to works listed in the selective bibliography at the end of this volume are by an italicised number in parentheses, followed, wherever appropriate, by a page number, e.g.: (*34,* p. 31).

My thanks to Celia Britton, Hanya Naït-Ladjemil, and Geoffrey Strickland, and to Professor Roger Little as Advisory Editor.

S.P.

Introduction

LEGEND has it that the 1967 winner of the Prix Fémina learnt of the prize's existence only when told she was being considered for it. Winning it, in the words of Simone de Beauvoir, 'lui a permis de se monter une garde-robe – elle ne possédait qu'un seul chandail – et de quitter le taudis où elle habitait' (*8*, p. 64). It also, of course, meant instant fame. It is rare for a major literary prize to be awarded for a first novel – or to an ex-Citroën worker with a minimum of formal education (and one jersey). The media sensed a good story.

Some seven weeks earlier the newly published *Elise ou la vraie vie* (henceforth *Elise*) had received a very favourable review from André Dalmas in *Le Monde* and so impressed Claude Lanzmann [1] that he had ordered Beauvoir to read it, knowing that once she had she would want to interview the writer. Now the television, radio and other journals were eager to talk to Claire Etcherelli, both about the novel itself and her reaction to the critics' appraisal of it.

From the articles and interviews published at this time it is clear that the Denoël press releases stressed how much more limited than had been thought was the role of autobiography. Yes, Etcherelli had lost her father (but not her mother) in the war; yes, she had left Bordeaux for Paris and work on the assemblyline at a car manufacturer's where the majority of the workers were North-African immigrants. But she was not an orphan; had not been brought up by a grandmother; had no brother; and was already the divorced mother of a young son when she took up work at the Citroën plant. (A few more details would emerge with the publication of Beauvoir's *Tout compte fait* in 1972.)

Contemporary interviews also convey a certain sense of bewilderment on the part of the authoress. Jean Gaugeard asked

[1] He would go on to collaborate with director Michel Drach on the film adaptation of the novel.

if the reception of her novel had surprised her: 'Ce qui frappe le plus les lecteurs d'*Elise* c'est apparemment ce que je dis de la vie en usine. Et cela est vraiment un peu extraordinaire. Les gens vivent en pleine société industrielle et si vous leur parlez de l'usine, ils tombent des nues' (*4*). Furthermore, she added, the critics had concentrated not on the style but on 'l'anecdote d'*Elise*'. Etcherelli's frustration is plain: her novel was, in her opinion, being praised for its documentary qualities, its 'fly on the wall' look at shop-floor racism and immigrant misery/factory working conditions/women in modern industrial society. All of which a sociological study could quite adequately have described. A grammar-enthusiast and avid reader who had started writing at 13 and whose favourite author was Balzac, Etcherelli had a passion for literature (having read her way through several suburban libraries) and had sought to write a *novel,* to create a work of artistic merit. Her book was however being hailed more as an account; a fictionalised, 1960s version of Simone Weil's unique 'Journal d'usine' (to which we shall return in chapters 2 and 3). And this she explained to Francine Mallet: 'J'ai admiré la façon dont Simone de Beauvoir m'a posé, au sujet du travail féminin, les questions qu'il fallait, mais par contre j'ai été déçue que tous les critiques de mon livre se soient attachés presque exclusivement à ce point de vue. Si j'avais voulu parler seulement de la condition des femmes à l'usine ou du racisme, j'aurais écrit une chronique. Or j'ai choisi la forme du roman parce que je tenais à créer des personnages, à les faire vivre, et parce que j'attache beaucoup d'importance à l'écriture' (*5*).

It would of course have been ludicrous not to discuss the novel's depiction and examination of racism and its horrors; the question, then, is one of degree. From the nineties we can see how soon after the Algerian declaration of independence October 1967 'really' was; we also know what was to come to the surface the following spring. Critics' concentration on the issues of racial strife and worker unrest was inevitable. Only the Anglo Saxon reviewers, who had merely watched the war their French counterparts had lived, would tend more towards viewing the novel as a whole. The anonymous *Times Literary Supplement* reviewer is a case in point. (S)he at least discussed character development and the qualities of the writing before concluding that 'The second half of the book is of enormous documentary interest as well' (*6*). But then (s)he was, as a later comment underlines, an outside observer: 'Here is a view of the Algerian war, and the Parisian atmosphere of viciousness and hysteria it evoked, that must be relatively new to many readers in this country'.

The hindsight that comes from knowledge of an author's later work also helps put this novel and its preoccupations in perspective. *A propos de Clémence* (1971), with its world of poor Spanish refugees, and *Un arbre voyageur* (1978), which continues the chronological scheme and depicts the build-up to May '68 as experienced by the protagonist Milie, confirm Etcherelli as a writer for whom the political climate acts as springboard and writing as 'l'arme d'un combat' (*18*). While unsure of its *efficacy* in the sense of its propagandist value – 'je suis sceptique sur le rôle de l'écriture, sur la puissance du livre' – she nevertheless believes in the value of art as testimony: 'il n'est pas inutile de témoigner ce qu'a pu être la condition réelle des individus dans une situation politique donnée' (*18*). The knowledge that these three works were originally conceived of as forming a trilogy, *Des années noires,* and that a fourth, dealing with '68-'72 and Maoist influence, was envisaged, allows today's reader to see the decrying of racial prejudice in a novel set during the middle years of the Algerian war within the perspective of a larger body of work, each component of which deals with different forms of social and political unrest. The atmosphere of fear and the racial tension was for Etcherelli what characterised that period of France's history (just as Milie's exhilaration and her welcoming of 'l'enfant de mai' translate Etcherelli's own perception of the spirit of May '68). Such a climate had therefore to play a major role in her book if it were to reply to her own conception and demands of the novel.

But in 1967 the portrayal of that climate was the major attribute of the novel to contemporary reviewers who admired it – and generally the major defect for those who did not. Coming a close second as main virtue to its treatment of racism was its portrayal of work on the assembly line, the slice-of-(proletarian)-life aspect. And it was the exploration of the role of women in industrial society that had been the main talking point of the pre-Fémina interview with Beauvoir. The novel was concerned, therefore, with not one but several of the most important issues of the day – something that Michel Drach, whose film-adaptation was released some three years later, was at pains to underline: '*Elise* pose les problèmes du travail à la chaîne, du travail des femmes, des "cadences infernales", de l'émigration, du racisme' (*19*). And while holding such issues up to the light it systematically revealed realities behind many of the relevant stereotypes that for various reasons the press, public and political parties held so dear.

All of which characteristics, laudable as they may be, are not in themselves sufficient to explain the esteem in which the novel came to be held. The mere fact of making of a time's greatest ills the material for a creative work is no guarantee of artistic quality. *Guernica* is not a great painting because of the destruction of Guernica; were I to sketch child prostitutes in Manilla no work of distinction would be produced. Some reviews of *Elise* stressed its 'authenticité', 'pudeur', 'dignité' (*12; 4; 7,* p. 145); Christian Melchior-Bonnet, while significantly rejecting any political message, nevertheless praised it highly for its 'sincérité' and 'sobriété', and concluded that '*Si on laisse de côté certains éléments politiques,* on trouve ici un vrai son humain' (*14,* p. 319; my stress). The creation and maintaining of the clear, spare style that is the hallmark voice of Elise; the skilful exploitation of the limiting first-person narrative; the investigation of the mysteries of sibling dependence; the portrayal of the halting beginning and abrupt end of a love affair . . . such are some of the attributes, somewhat neglected on the novel's first appearance, which contribute to the complexity, authenticity and success of this novel. What is perceived as ideological merit has been allowed to overshadow its artistic merit but should not be permitted to deny it. While a discussion of major themes as noted by most critics is naturally indispensable I hope also in this study in a small way to help redress the balance.

1

Franco-Algerian Relations

TO-ING AND FRO-ING

FROM 1830, when Charles X took Algiers, until then under Turkish control, for France, emigration in both directions in response to various economic and political promptings was a vital factor in the relationship between metropolitan France and the three *départements* Algeria would quickly come to constitute.

In Algeria, once resistance to the French invasion had been put down (1847), colonisation was encouraged, with Algerian land being meted out in lots to the French 'immigrants'. The Second Republic made Algeria part of French territory; under the Second Empire, colonisation continued, with the colonists vetoing many moves designed to improve the living standards of the indigenous population. The speedily quashed Muslim rebellion in 1871, together with France's desire to become a force to be reckoned with in the Mediterranean, and her loss of Alsace-Lorraine to Prussia, refuelled the colonial fire: from 1872 to the outbreak of World War One, the European population of Algeria tripled.

In France, the earliest wave of Algerian immigrants – mostly poor farm labourers from the mountain villages of Greater Kabylia – found work in the 1880s around the Marseilles docks. With the outbreak of war they were repatriated, but in 1915 their labour was required in French munitions factories and mines. Although some returned to Algeria at the end of the war, emigration to France continued through the twenties, dwindling during the thirties' slump but then increasing until the outbreak of World War Two. In 1945, French reconstruction demanded a considerable workforce; the immigration this encouraged continued unabated until 1954, and the beginning of the Algerian war.

The fifties

In 1954, the UIMM (Union des Industries Mécaniques et Minières de la Construction Mécanique, Electrique et Métallique) 'reported the presence . . . of 300,000 Algerian workers' (*31,* p. 57), 80 % of whom were from rural areas. Having no knowledge of heavy industry, no training, and often little spoken and no written French, these workers could only seek the job of labourer *(manœuvre)* or semi-skilled worker grade 1 *(ouvrier spécialisé 1)*. The construction industry and the motor industry in particular benefited from a workforce prepared to accept the manual jobs French workers themselves were increasingly loath to take.

For the immigrants the transition period was often both brutal and bewildering. Taken on only for the poorest paid, most dangerous, dirty and arduous jobs, usually badly housed, almost always sending a portion of the weekly wage home to ensure the upkeep of family and lands, they were often condemned, by their poor command of French, to loneliness and confusion. (And in most cases that linguistic deficiency meant that they could not attend training courses to better their lot.) Etcherelli paints a grim picture (see in particular p. 208/223) of the life of the Algerian immigrant; also writing in the sixties, Ahsène Zehraoui conducted a survey on the family life of Algerian workers in France, and was given vivid descriptions of the problems of adaptation experienced during the first few months in Paris: 'Pour me rendre à mon travail, je prenais des grains de pois chiches avec lesquels je comptais les stations', and again: 'Je ne parvenais pas à m'exprimer dans la langue française. Quelquefois je me perdais dans le métro et je m'orientais difficilement dans les rues. Certains jours, cela durait des heures et personne ne pouvait m'aider' (*32,* p. 86).

The climate

Post-colonial racism is a particularly pernicious phenomenon, suffering as it does from 'toutes les conséquences qu'impliquaient les relations dominé-dominant, exploiteur-exploité' (*32,* p. 250). (In 1954 there were twice as many Italians as Algerians in France, and some 75,000 more Spaniards; little hostility, however, was or is directed against these Catholic European neighbours whose culture and languages have so much in common with those of the French.) Its invidious stereotyping can at times seem impervious to the facts: thus the considerable role played by the Algerian workers in France's economic development is regularly disparaged and the image of the immigrant worker 'qui mange le pain des Français' persists.

A 1955 UIMM report debunked in no uncertain terms the 'lazy North African' stereotype, managing at the same time to query the assiduity of the French worker:

> Prejudices concerning absenteeism and accidents, where everyone thinks that the North African is more often sick, has more accidents and absents himself more often, do not stand up to analysis when we know that they do the most dangerous manual jobs and that they live in privation. In spite of all this, it is surprising to observe that total absenteeism among North Africans is no greater than among Europeans. (*31,* p. 113)

But unpublicised official documents such as these do little to counteract stereotypical images of Algerians of the kind Etcherelli is at pains to contradict in *Elise.* From 1954 to the end of the war (and, for some, beyond it), Algerians were in any case the immigrant enemy – and as such, for those areas of the media that so willed it, fair game.

THE BUILD-UP TO WAR

In an article entitled 'Algeria: The Tortured Conscience', Chester W. Obuchowski remarks, with considerable understatement, that this was 'a fantastically complex war' (*29,* p. 91). It was indeed complex, not only politically, but also on the level of personal loyalties. Its seeds had, after all, been sown precisely one and a quarter centuries previously, and now its roots ran very deep.

French colonisation of Algeria had introduced the kinds of modifications European colonists considered synonymous with civilisation. Roads were constructed, schools built, railway tracks laid. Improvements in medical facilities meant that the infant mortality rate dropped; competition in the work place meant that many indigenous craftsmen had to seek alternative employment. As the population grew, the standard of living of native Algerians therefore tended to drop.

By 1930, and the centenary celebrations, Algeria's population thus comprised: ever-increasing numbers of increasingly poor non-European natives (mostly Arab, but also including the Berbers of the North, with their own language and non-Islamic culture); an élite of this population, educated in French-run establishments; and the colonists, or the descendants of the colonists, the *pieds noirs* – European Algerians, born in Algeria, some, like Albert Camus, being the second or third generation to call Algeria their native country.

Moves for reform, for an improvement in the standard of living and the political rights of non-European Algerians, were made in 1936 when issues such as joint French-Muslim citizenship were discussed. The French community in Algeria caused these bids to fail, this reaction setting the pattern for years to come. By World War Two, which saw Algerian soldiers triumphing in Italy, and France's loss of prestige following her defeat, several nationalist movements existed in Algeria, all demanding change. The various minor reforms they caused to be instigated, and which might have pacified a pre-war Algeria, were far from being adequate now. In May 1945 a demonstration at Sétif left some one hundred Europeans dead; in the reprisal action, literally tens of thousands of non-European Algerians were arrested, imprisoned, tortured, killed. The support for nationalist movements grew, the majority choosing between the Islamic cultural fundamentalist Messali Hadj's Mouvement pour le Triomphe des Libertés Démocratiques (MTLD), and the moderate Ferhat Abbas's Union Démocratique du Manifeste d'Alger (UDMA: named after a manifesto calling for an autonomous Algerian state under French protection).

So – poverty, misery and the secret planning of rebellion: this is Algeria during Elise's early twenties, and she, like most of the rest of France, is unaware of it all; France had after all been fighting a colonial war in Indochina since 1946, and that has had no effect on her life: 'On s'y battait, mais je ne m'en souciais pas' (p. 15/60). At first even Lucien's obsession with it doesn't awaken her curiosity:

> –Ils sont à fond contre la guerre.
> –Quelle guerre? Tout le monde est contre la guerre.
> –Tu crois? Tu ne sais pas que depuis cinq ans on se bat?
> –Ah mais en Indochine! (p. 21/65)

It is the Elise of the novel's true present who comments in retrospect on the lack of concern she felt when Lucien brought home the pacifist journal: 'Je me souviens de quel ton léger je lui dis cela. Une guerre lointaine, discrète, aux causes imprécises, presque rassurante, une preuve de bonne santé, de vitalité' (p. 21/65).

In 1954 Lucien becomes a father, Henri comes back into their lives, and in May the war whose progress Elise is now following in the press enters its death throes with the fall of Dien Bien Phu, a defeat which shook the army and would later influence its behaviour in Algeria. Also in 1954, convinced by Dien Bien Phu that direct action was their only option, ex members of the MTLD, out of sympathy with Messali Hadj's extreme fundamentalism, formed the FLN (Front de Libération Nationale).

Algeria in 1954 had a population of some $9^{1}/_{2}$ million, of which 10 % were of European (mainly French) origin. Of that 10 %, four fifths were born in Algeria. The non-European population was experiencing 25 % unemployment; there was therefore a sizeable Algerian population in France, including many Berbers, driven to leave their mountain villages to find work. As plans to fight for independence grew, they met with support from Algerians in France, where the Berbers turned to the FLN and its stress on Algerian (not Arabic) and democratic (not Muslim) aims. In October 1954 the FLN in Algeria attacked the French military and government buildings. Algeria's war for independence had officially begun.

The war and Elise

For Elise's immediate circle, within which only she and Lucien have followed the Indochinese war, events in Algeria, or even in Paris, mean little. Henri, prior to going to the capital, arrives one evening with a newspaper: 'Il nous jeta un nom auquel je ne prêtai pas attention; ce nom, c'était l'Algérie' (p. 47/87). It is through Lucien that Elise learns of the turn events are taking; Henri gone, it is to her that he talks of 'le racisme en Afrique du Nord, jusqu'à quel excès il se porte . . . mais on a honte, certains sévices ne laissent aucune trace' (p. 47/87).

Those 'sévices', brutal systematic acts of torture, were racking Algeria, the French army being determined to put down (this) rebellion, the FLN determined to achieve independence. The European population was fearful; the non-Europeans were petrified by the FLN but hated the French notion of regrouping villagers in *zones de sécurité*. In France, where esteemed figures such as Sartre were proclaiming their support for the FLN, more reform bills were blocked by colonist pressure. Disillusioned, Ferhat Abbas too joined the FLN. Atrocities became everyday events; brutal FLN attacks upon Europeans and on villages suspected of harbouring French sympathisers drew swift reprisals from the army, which had, as one veteran pointed out to Obuchowski, a dual role: 'one day he would come bringing bonbons and medicine to the Moslem villagers and, on the next, he would be back with a list of suspects in his pocket and a grenade in his hand' (*29,* p. 91). The French Communist Party now allowed members as individuals to support the FLN: the fundamentalist Messali Hadj made much of this Communist support in his anti-FLN propaganda, and fighting between members of the two nationalist parties was rife, both in Algeria and in France (centering in Paris on the Goutte d'Or area where Arezki lives).

All of this Lucien and Elise follow in the press and in Henri's letters. 'La guerre', says Elise hopelessly to Lucien, 'Il faut faire quelque chose' (p. 47/88). But it still remains abstract to her, almost a secret that only she and her brother share. Indeed Lucien's wife knows little about world events, and less about 'la mentalité raciste qui se développait furieusement' (p. 54/93) – but she recognises that, devoting himself to a cause, he is abandoning her and their daughter. 'Moi aussi je suis ton Algérie' (p. 55/95), Marie-Louise tells her husband, who is discomfited by her perceptiveness. Lucien will leave for Paris with that 'Algérie' ringing in his ears; following him there, Elise will exchange what we may term an informed interest for an involvement beyond her imaginings. Her claustrophobic home-background has been carefully detailed; the reader is aware that, in going to Paris, Elise is leaving a town with no significant immigrant population, a job – typing from home – which brought her into contact with very few people, and a particularly small circle of family and friends. She is even taking the train for the first time. Objectively, Elise understands the situation that Algerian immigrants in Paris face at this moment, but she has no notion of the climate of resentment and aggression that reigns there, and the overt racism she will meet when she takes work at the car-manufacturing plant.

2

Racism

BEFORE Elise's first day of factory work (occurring a third of the way into the novel) she has never personally witnessed an instance of racist behaviour – what she knows of anti-Algerian feeling comes from the preconceived ideas of her grandmother and her reading of the press. Beginning with the day she is taken on at the car manufacturer's, she is confronted with a variety of situations which will force her to review certain notions she has taken as given. Her experiences are designed to do the same for the reader, who is throughout the novel prompted to examine his stance on various issues. These get progressively more complex as the plot of the novel and Elise's relationship with Arezki develop.

What, then, does Elise record of that first day? First the queue of mainly immigrant workers on whom the *gardien* closes the door 'vivement' both actually and figuratively, since sending him away jobless certainly shut a door for an unemployed North-African in Paris in 1958. The aggressive *tutoiement* the *gardien* employs; his shouting; the fact that he seems capable only of contradicting ('On n'embauche pas', p. 74/109) or interrogating those seeking work – all this makes for what is a new and disturbing experience for Elise. At this point no narrative comment intervenes; the hostility is instantly underlined as the *gardien*'s treatment of Elise is contrasted with it. We are shown that he lied (the factory is taking on hands, but selectively); that Elise automatically merits *vouvoiement;* and that doors shut in the faces of immigrants are opened for white French nationals.

Next Elise goes for the medical examination. The overheard comment of the doctor addressing the worker in front of her: 'Tu t'appelles Mohammed? [. . .] Tous les Arabes s'appellent Mohammed' (p. 75/110) instantly debunks one belief her discussions with Lucien and Henri will have held as self-evident, which is that only the ignorant and poorly-educated are racially prejudiced. This highly-educated professional, holding a position of authority and influence, sees no reason to treat Arabs as individuals – and every reason to warn Elise against staying with them on the assembly line. His jovial manner and apparent concern for her welfare shock more than the simple disdain of the *gardien*.

Declared fit, Elise can proceed to workshop 76, where she is given into the charge of one of its few French workers, Daubat. He does not welcome this new turn of events: 'C'est les femmes, maintenant?' (p. 78/112), he queries ruefully. But when an Arab worker echoes that same observation to him, Daubat is most brusque: 'Oui, et après? Travaille, t'as déjà une voiture de retard' (p. 80/114). At lunchtime Daubat predicts that Elise will take a while to get into the work routine, 'D'autant qu'avec les ratons c'est pas facile' (p. 82/115). 'Ratons', 'bicots', 'crouillats' – such terms punctuate Daubat's conversation, and his unselfconscious use of them indicates that he takes it for granted that Elise shares both that vocabulary and the attitudes it reveals. As do the other French workers who, with Daubat, present themselves to Elise as gallant knights a damsel can call on should the immigrant workers distress her ('Nous sommes là', p. 86/118). As the afternoon shift begins, Daubat draws Elise's attention to an Arab cat-napping on a pile of fibre-glass sheets, and asks rhetorically: 'Vous croyez que ce sont des hommes? Ils ont de la corne à la place de peau' (p. 86/119). The immigrants are then not only of another race – they belong to another species, are not human at all.

Debunked, exploded, here is another myth held dear by Lucien (originally), Elise and the Left in general. The idealism holding worker solidarity to be more deeply entrenched than racism is in this novel repeatedly shown to be delusion, illusion. With regard to the racist issue, Etcherelli is concerned specifically to destroy popular – and political – myth. To show up preconception as misconception she creates a newly-aware but simultaneously naïve protagonist who finds that the definite lines of her own reasoned, informed stance blur as she experiences its practical implications.

Significantly, however, Etcherelli is careful to show Elise's sensitivity towards those discriminated against grow prior to her relationship with Arezki, developing through her observations of her work-mates, discussions with Lucien, etc. The first conversation with Mustapha, for example, disturbs Elise because she realises that he has misconstrued her reserve as being a manifestation of racist sentiment. Although this misunderstanding is soon cleared up, Elise remains permanently confused as to how best to mark a solidarity with the Algerians which the French workers regard as misplaced and the immigrants themselves seem to resent. When she lets past some of Mustapha's shoddy workmanship neither he nor Gilles is pleased, and Elise is bewildered: 'l'un comme l'autre, ils étaient mécontents. Mais que faire? Etre dure . . .?' (p. 108/138). The danger of appearing patronising looms close; Elise is learning that a simplistic black and white, for or against approach over-simplifies a complex, nuanced situation.

She is also being brought towards a realisation that her own conscious rejection of racism is constantly assailed by new external factors. One example can be found in the newspaper headlines which, despite her intellectual appreciation of the press's power to manipulate and distort, retain their ability to influence her judgement: 'Dans l'autobus, autour de moi, il y avait beaucoup d'Algériens. Etaient-ils du FLN? Tuaient-ils la nuit?' (p. 90/123). The newspapers' crude illustrations are equally impressive, the sketches of secret FLN juries and their victims ensuring the hostility and maintaining the fear of the French, and lingering in Elise's mind as she scrutinises her fellow-workers; Arab brutality, Arab aggression – what the population wants now to believe, the press is confirming.

Another major myth debunked by Etcherelli is that of the Arab Animal, the highly-sexed protagonist of the strip-cartoon 'La passion du Maure' that a previous girlfriend of Arezki's was wont to read (p. 159/182). On her first day at the factory the hooting and wolf-whistles which frighten Elise are explained to her by Lucien – 'A travailler comme ça, on retourne à l'état animal. Des bestiaux qui voient la femelle' (p. 83/116) – and later by Arezki: 'L'usine, ça rend sauvages' (p. 102/133). The cries also have something defiant in them. Despite the dirty, exhausting work, the workers will not become machines incapable of responding; thus explained, their reactions arouse pity. Elise's own preconceptions are soon underlined, the better to be shown up for the misjudgements they are: 'Imprégnée d'idées reçues, j'avais pensé [. . .] ça y est, maintenant, il va m'emmener dans sa chambre. Mais rien ne s'était produit. Notre accord était un miracle. Tout autre que lui se serait montré plus impatient et plus audacieux' (p. 182/201).

The racist 'angle' of the novel widens a few notches at a time. From Henri's first reference to Algeria, Lucien's reading and the meetings he attends, all of which are discussed with her, Elise moves to the working environment of the car factory and thence 'deeper into' the issue as her friendship with Arezki grows. Her first experience of having a drink with an Algerian fills her with panic; fear paralyses her as she watches her first police swoop at an underground entrance; Arezki's swarthiness shocks her when glimpsed suddenly in the bright lights and hostile environment of a café ('Mon Dieu, qu'il avait l'air arabe!', p. 156/179). Her secret distances her definitively from the women she works with and destroys any hope of making friends of them; when a moment of pique causes her to refuse an invitation from Arezki, she recognises that the women have in a subtle way, and all unknowing, influenced her decision – and that her feelings for Arezki are growing: 'Vous êtes pour quelque chose dans ce non. J'ai peur de vous toutes. Mais le thé chaud, le contact de sa main quand il me quitte, et cette marche dans la nuit, je ne peux pas y renoncer' (p. 174/194). And while depicting the pressures under which a Franco-Algerian couple operated in Paris in 1957, Etcherelli continues her methodic demystification of those cherished generalisations highlighted earlier, and those preconceptions she bestows in particular upon Elise. Elise thinks that Arezki is exaggerating when he sees police everywhere, Elise thinks that provided one's papers are in order there is nothing to fear from police questioning . . . such naïvety is soon corrected.

With Lucien's revelation, the 'angle' widens further as we see Elise trying to come to terms with the difference in attitude of Bernier, the other workers, the women in the cloakroom. Sly allusions are made or Elise is simply ignored: the point is underlined that racial distrust creates a stronger bond than sexual solidarity. Once the relationship is no longer secret within the factory it cannot remain so outside it; Etcherelli can thus extend Elise's circle of acquaintances, allowing her to meet Arezki's pathetic, intimidated uncle and his militant colleagues at Nanterre. Now an outcast among her 'own kind' at work, Elise is similarly an outsider at the Nanterre meetings: the language is a barrier; Arezki's friends are sceptical about her interest in their cause; and her naïvety again stresses the gulf between theory and reality (in a world where Algerians daily go missing without trace Elise is indignant that Mustapha should not be able to express his anger at Daubat's racist remarks). When finally she and Arezki have a chance of privacy in his Goutte d'Or lodgings, the police swoop further reinforces the notion of the outcast: like the less-than-human worker asleep on the fibre-glass, the white Frenchwoman found in an Arab's room is also *not human*: 'Tu appelles ça des femmes!' (p. 218/232). The parallel is deftly made and most striking.

Finally the immigrants' impromptu 'concert' at the factory stresses the Africans' 'otherness' ('si l'on n'était pas dans le secret, dans la magie de cette musique, on ne pouvait y entrer sans se trouver à contretemps, sans cesse à contretemps', p. 235/246), and brings home to Elise the kind of truth ('Rien ne ferait jamais admettre à Daubat, au régleur, à bien d'autres, que les norafs étaient leurs égaux', p. 236/247) which she cannot countenance accepting, and which she thus rejects in favour of idealistic illusion: 'Un jour, il n'y aurait pas besoin de chambre où nous cacher'. But the moment of euphoria ends abruptly with another illustration of the power of the *idée reçue.* Daubat has pointed out to Mustapha the damage his tapping feet have done to the car's paintwork:

> Mustapha, encore ivre, le saisit au col de son bleu.
> –Si tu le dis au contremaître, je t'attends à la sortie, je t'ouvre le ventre et je te mange la viande.
> L'autre avait pâli. Il y croyait. (p. 237/247)

Knowing that Daubat believes such notions Mustapha plays on and therefore reinforces the image of the 'wild beast' – why not for once merit such a reputation?

In this and the following novels, Etcherelli reveals a mistrust of fine words and unbuttered parsnips as proffered by both right- and left-wing thought. In *Elise,* the communist foreman Gilles is portrayed as a sensitive and sympathetic character, but on the issue of worker racism disappoints Elise by falling back on the 1958 party line, a line which appeared to Etcherelli and appears to Elise insincere and unconvincing.

> –Si le bicot n'existait pas, on inventerait quelqu'un d'autre. Comprenez, face à l'Arabe, ils s'affirment. Ajoutez l'ignorance, l'inculture, la peur de ce qui ne vous ressemble pas, la guerre par là-dessus . . . Tout cela, il faut l'extirper habilement par un long et patient travail et non par l'action brutale, directe et anarchique.
>
> Il ne m'avait pas convaincue. (p. 241/251)

Gilles himself seems uncomfortable with this attitude and contents himself by sententiously concluding 'Je suis d'accord avec des décisions qui ont été pesées, analysées et discutées' (p. 241/251). His awareness that the Communist Party was above all concerned with not alienating white working-class support is apparent, as is Elise's view that this is an inadequate reponse. But both characters, together with Lucien and Anna, 'persuadés que l'heure était enfin venue' (p. 258/266), are carried away by what Gilles fondly sees as the spirit of worker solidarity which follows the May 13th uprising in Algiers. Because of the demonstration planned for the 28th, Arezki agrees to visit Elise the evening prior to it. He doesn't, and the next day Elise reads of Lucien's death.

Reeling from the news, Elise sets out to bury her brother, stopping in the Goutte d'Or area to seek an explanation for Arezki's three-day absence. She learns from the lodger who has already taken over his room that the police have detained him. 'La révolution est un bulldozer', Arezki had said, 'Elle passe'.

Elise recalls the image as she goes in turn to see Ferhat, Mustapha and Slimane. For such as these 'La disparition d'Arezki était naturelle, elle s'inscrivait dans une fatale logique dont j'étais la seule à m'émouvoir' (p. 273/278). It is the obscenity of such a logic that the novel sets out to illustrate.

3

Working-Class Witness

> *Règlement intérieur du Creusot, 30 avril 1964:*
> Article 15: Il est défendu aux ouvriers de l'Usine . . . 4°) de former des groupes sans autorisation, de chanter, et de se livrer à des manifestations quelconques. (*34*, p. 72).

'QUALIFIER sa prose de littérature prolétarienne', Bernard Alliot has written of Claire Etcherelli, 'relève d'une classification réductrice'. The categorisation is for Alliot only 'réductrice', however, as the completed comment stresses, if one is using the term to designate what are merely bald accounts: 'réductrice, si l'on désigne une écriture brute, un texte de témoignage sans recherche esthétique' (*20*).

The clause serves to highlight the problem inherent in using labels such as 'littérature prolétarienne', or indeed 'populaire/populiste/ouvrière', which is that many conflicting definitions of such terms have been put forward, and various cases made for each. It is as well briefly to look at what has gone before, and to weigh the respective merits of 'by' or 'of' or 'about' the working class, before considering Alliot's point.

The living and working conditions of the big city poor have been charted by some of the world's greatest authors, Balzac contrasting the excesses of Parisian highlife with the misery of those it fed off, Dickens giving us the underbelly of London. Works about the proletariat (written by members of another class) have proliferated since the industrial revolution created the industrial worker: Zola's *L'Assommoir* (1877), set in the Goutte d'Or district, provoked outrage with its depiction of Paris's poor; his *Germinal* (1884) brought the life of the coal-miner into middle-class drawing rooms.

By the 1920s, interest in literature depicting such milieux gave birth to the Ecole populiste (founded in 1929). Its founder, Léon Lemonnier, defined his stance thus:

> La littérature populiste n'est pas nécessairement faite *par* le peuple. Elle n'est pas non plus nécessairement faite *pour* le peuple. [. . .] Il vaudrait mieux certes, que l'une et l'autre conditions fussent remplies. Mais il peut suffire, à la rigueur, de prendre le peuple pour sujet. (*36,* pp. 181-85)

Created by writers who were themselves in the main of middle-class origin, this group sought to capture something of what it termed 'la pittoresque rudesse' of working-class life. The pitfalls attendant on such an approach – a tendency towards parody, towards romanticising, antisepticising, above all stereotyping – were swiftly pointed out by opponents of the populist movement, angry at what they saw as the appropriation of the domain of the proletariat by 'les romanciers bourgeois qui peignent le peuple par occasion' (*40,* p. 63). The Ecole prolétarienne that Henri Poulaille founded in 1932 would therefore promote works not simply *about* but *by* working people: 'La vie du prolétariat racontée par des auteurs qui sortent de ses rangs: voilà la littérature prolétarienne' (*40,* p. 66). And *its* shortcomings were in turn emphasised by detractors: the school was accused of allowing its goals of realism and authenticity to sway its critical judgement, of promoting any piece produced by a working-class writer regardless of literary merit. Furthermore, its credo comprehended something of a paradox, summed up here by Geneviève Bollème: 'L'ouvrier, le travailleur, le peuple écrivant, [. . .] en raison de la situation qui est la leur, se trouveront séparés d'une communauté à laquelle ils appartiennent et dont l'acte d'écrire les éloigne' (*33,* p. 246). The worker who becomes a *writer* is no longer a worker . . .

Moreover, the appropriate subject-matter for those aspiring to contribute to a true 'working-class literature' was similarly under dispute. Some maintained that a proletarian literature had by definition to oppose the literature of the (middle-class) establishment, to preach revolution – 'Littérature non-conformiste, littérature de combat, c'est par là seulement qu'elle peut prétendre se séparer nettement de la littérature bourgeoise' – while remaining apart from political considerations ('La littérature prolétarienne n'a que faire [. . .] des idéologies politiques', *38,* p. 41).

Others on the other hand criticised those who, albeit from undoubtedly laudable motives, encouraged working-class writers to limit themselves to writing barely fictionalised documentary: 'Longtemps, nous avons fait cette erreur de croire que les prolos écrivains devaient exclusivement écrire en "camarade syndiqué de la charrette à bras", qu'ils devaient se contenter de copier leur vie, sans plus, sans se permettre la moindre poétique, le moindre lyrisme' (*38,* p. 59). (Or, to echo Alliot, 'la moindre recherche esthétique'.)

Against this background appeared a steady stream of works portraying the life of the manual worker. Metallurgist Jean Pallu's *L'Usine* (1931) comprised a set of tableaux covering various aspects of factory life; it was followed in the year of Etcherelli's birth (1934) by *J'ai failli boucler la boucle,* with its depiction of a 'taylorised' factory (F. W. Taylor's *Principles of Scientific Organisation* had appeared in America in 1909). And in the December of 1934 Simone Weil took a job working in a Renault factory, thus beginning the experience which was to fuel her haunting 'Journal d'usine' and the letters and articles that with it make up *La Condition ouvrière.* The physical toll of the work undertaken, the constant fear – of arriving late, of not producing one's quota, of having an accident – colour this singular diary, but it is perhaps above all the numbing effect leading to the feeling that 'la révolte est impossible' (*42,* p. 68) which most shocks both Weil and the reader. A contemporaneous letter explains this in more detail: 'Ne crois pas qu'il en soit résulté en moi des mouvements de révolte. Non, mais au contraire la chose au monde que j'attendais le moins de moi-même – la docilité. Une docilité de bête de somme résignée. [. . .] Je ne suis pas fière d'avouer ça. C'est le genre de souffrance dont aucun ouvrier ne parle: ça fait trop mal même d'y penser' (*42,* p. 27).

With the post-war reconstruction projects occupying the economy and a large part of the workforce, it was not until the fifties that France began to build up industry, developing large industrial zones around major cities, moving within plants from the mechanised to the automatic. Journalist Roger Vailland's *325.000 francs* (1955) captures the spirit of the time; here his protagonist contemplates the automatic plastic press that has just been installed in the small family-run factory where he works:

Il réfléchissait qu'il coûtait moins cher qu'un dispositif d'automatisation. D'un côté le peigne éjecteur et l'œil électronique, de l'autre côté Bernard Busard, son grand corps maigre, ses muscles de coureur, son cerveau, son amour pour Marie-Jeanne Lemercier; c'était Bernard Busard qui valait le moins.

Il valait un peu plus qu'un piston injecteur et le servomoteur qui le meut, puisqu'on avait remplacé la presse à main par la presse semi-automatique. Mais il valait moins que la somme des prix de la presse semi-automatique et du dispositif d'automatisation intégrale. Son prix était inscrit entre deux limites bien précises. Il aurait pu calculer exactement ce qu'il valait d'argent. (*41*, p. 159)

If early works dealing with the industrial worker's living and working conditions concentrated above all, then, on the dirty, dangerous and exhausting nature of factory work, those that came later brought out something more: the dehumanising aspects of a machine-dominated world where the assembly line or 'le chrono' is God, and the hated 'cadences' rhythm one's life (Vailland makes a point of describing the workers' use of 'maxiton' or other amphetamines to keep them awake towards the end of a long shift). The knowledge that the most valued worker is the worker most able to emulate the machines surrounding him is shown to be if anything more debilitating than the work itself. Three years after the publication of *Elise* Philippe Gavi's *Les Ouvriers* appeared, the fruit of a nationwide enquiry into the lives of industrial workers in France. Towards the close of the book, exploring the notion of what makes a good worker, he is led to cite the Union Nationale des Associations de Parents d'Enfants Handicapés . . . and to draw from it a chilling conclusion:

A la différence du normal qui craint de devenir un rouage et de perdre sa personnalité dans un travail trop mécanique, le débile jouit de la puissance et de la force de la machine, consécration de son rôle, assouvissant ainsi son désir de domination. Il trouve dans le travail le sens de son existence et ce travail n'est ni un jeu ni une occupation . . .

> On peut se demander alors s'il faut être un débile mental pour être un bon ouvrier, ou si un bon ouvrier ne devient pas rapidement un débile mental. (*35,* p. 273)

Should we then shy away from the label of 'littérature prolétarienne' when discussing *Elise*? It is undeniable that the novel fulfils each of the various requirements for the category as defined by different schools and critics: it was written by a writer from the working-class, it treats a working-class environment, and Etcherelli's hopes concerning its potential readership offer a further glimpse of that environment: 'J'aimerais beaucoup être lue dans le monde du travail, évidemment, mais je sais que c'est très difficile. Les ouvriers lisent peu et mon livre est trop cher pour eux' (*3,* p. 28).

If it is then accurate to use the term 'littérature prolétarienne' when referring to Etcherelli's writing, it is accurate only when very broad definitions are agreed upon; Alliot is right to warn against other classifications which tend towards caricaturing *Elise* as the 'chronique' that Etcherelli herself felt critics were most interested in discussing. This is a novel – and from within that novel, the writer has certain things to say about the life of a factory worker in advanced industrial society. Her technique in *Elise* requires that the reader learn at the pace of the protagonist, who needs therefore to be ignorant of factory life until obliged to experience it. Hence Part 1 of the novel concentrates on establishing the social and economic context, showing the Letellier home life in Bordeaux. Despite the financial problems common to both, the provincial poverty ashamed of itself and desperate to keep up appearances contrasts sufficiently with the working life she is to know in Paris for the difference in the two life-styles to have a profound effect on Elise.

It is early apparent that the teenage Elise, taking in typing at home, feels privileged in comparison to many of her peers: 'je me jugeais favorisée en comparaison des filles de mon quartier qui, à quinze ans, prenaient le chemin de l'usine' (p. 12/57). The figurative use of 'chemin', comparable to the English 'road' as in 'road to ruin', underlines the fact that this is seen by Elise as a dead-end. The factory is of course where Marie-Louise works;

early in the novel, Elise dispassionately describes her day in one sentence: 'Elle se levait tôt, partait avant sept heures pour la biscuiterie, où jusqu'au soir, elle restait debout devant sa machine' (p. 23/67). A bald, flat account – but then Elise, trying to cope with the jealousy a sister-in-law's presence has awoken in her, has at this stage no interest in factory life.

Gradually, however, as her sympathy for that sister-in-law increases, Elise begins to admire 'l'héroïque Marie-Louise', the principal wage-earner of the household, always up at six to go to the factory where, until evening, she is 'rivée à sa machine' (p. 40/82). But both the pace and nature of the work, and Lucien's indifference, finally undermine Marie-Louise's health; she is packed off with her daughter to convalesce, leaving her husband free to pursue his ambitions. Because of what Etcherelli has chosen to make Marie-Louise – a factory worker – Lucien's abandoning of her is more than a little ironic. It is after all to be his own experience of factory life that shapes his belief in, and hopes for, socialism, and which draws from Henri the impatient, 'Tu es devenu ouvriériste' (p. 97/128); but the fact of having been married to a factory worker, and thus of knowing something of the working conditions and long hours, seems quite simply to have passed Lucien by.

Constraints lifted, Lucien heads for the capital. A few weeks after his arrival, he writes to tell Elise that he has taken a factory job. Anne Ophir has suggested that he has by this stage been working about a month in the factory (*15,* p. 180): both the idealism of the pompous opening line, where Lucien talks of 'un boulot pénible mais combien exaltant' (p. 58/97), and the repetition of the future tense, would seem to militate against his having worked there (so?) long. The naïvety of his stated aims is similarly not commensurate with his having experienced much of factory life: 'quand j'aurai fini la journée d'usine, je retrouverai mes papiers, mes cahiers [. . .] je témoignerai pour ceux qui ne peuvent le faire' (p. 59/97).

It is of course only later that the naïvety of such an aim will become apparent – to Lucien himself, to Elise, to the majority of readers. Later Elise will detail her exhaustion after a day's work; later, Lucien will try to explain such feelings to the uncomprehending Henri. For the present Lucien's efforts appear to his sister noble, and his dreams realisable; flattered by his attention, she leaves for Paris. Etcherelli gives an indication of what Elise will encounter there by prefacing the second part of the novel with an extract from Desnos's 'Hommes', which evokes the exhaustion, dirt, lack of energy and hopelessness that will find an echo in accounts of Elise's own working days.

Lucien's appearance the evening he proposes that Elise stay a while in Paris and take work at the factory aptly illustrates the toll factory work is taking on him; Etcherelli is giving an insight into effects before dwelling in any detail on the cause. Lucien is hollow-cheeked, weak, and filthy with ingrained dirt. He preempts any comment from his sister, echoing the Desnos poem, prefiguring Elise's own experience: 'Je suis si fatigué que je ne pense qu'à dormir. Je me laverai demain' (p. 66/101). In fact no comment is necessary: Elise's account of her own first day at the factory will prove comment enough.

On that first day the factory is, to Elise staring up at it, 'un immense mur et d'immenses portes de fer' (p. 73/107). Windows are painted out or covered with a grill: this is, in short, a prison. This daunting visual image before us, we move inside, and to the heavy doors muffling the ominous rumblings from workshop 76. Already trembling apprehensively, Elise is now deafened, and the workshop itself takes on mythical stature: '[Gilles] dit quelque chose, mais je ne pouvais plus l'entendre, j'étais *dans l'atelier 76*' (p. 76/110; my italics).

In this world of the nightmare, where everything is distorted, we *as*cend into horror (and later *de*scend to attain the paradise of the light, clear infirmary); workshop 76, where reigns a cacophony so frightful that Elise's first telling thought is that there has been a sudden accident, is, as the qualifiers ('déchirants', 'infernaux') stress, Hell. Almost immediately Elise sees 'un serpent de voitures' (p. 77/111), and lurking in the depths is the 'grand boa' (p. 120/148) that is the assembly line. Elise's job will entail jumping on and off this mechanical monster to check the car-carcasses carried along 'sur son ventre' (p. 78/112).

On her first day she finds the task very difficult; the noise literally stuns her. During the lunch break she sees the outside world with new, euphoric/hysterical eyes; it is left to Lucien to articulate what she is beginning to sense: 'la vie de l'ouvrier, elle commence à l'instant où finit le travail' (p. 84/117). Resuming after lunch, Elise is at first able to concentrate on and understand Gilles's explanations, and even ask for an explanation of what happens to the car body at earlier stages in its manufacture. But Gilles has not the time to explain. Elise is anyway beginning to tire; and from this point on the physical effect upon her of this work is brought out. A long (8-line) sentence mainly composed of infinitives of verbs of motion details the separate actions of the exhausting work. By the end of the afternoon Elise is even robbed of speech: 'je n'arrivais plus à articuler les mots' (p. 89/121). To complete this description of Elise's first day, Etcherelli moves into the narrative present for the final paragraphs, lending Elise's fatigue immediacy, and allowing her more faithfully (from a grammatical point of view) to echo her brother's exhaustion: 'Je me laverai tout à l'heure' (p. 90/122).

Although sharper because this environment is new to her, Elise's experience is that of all the workers, and, while specifically following her progress, we are given glimpses of how regular hands cope: taking naps at lunchtime, skimping on their work to snatch a few minutes for a cigarette. As the novel progresses, various days are picked out for comment; we see Elise noting correspondingly more about her workmates and surroundings as she gets into the work routine. By day 4 she is asking Daubat why newcomers are not shown round so that they see the whole manufacturing process and understand the role they are to play in it. (Simone Weil had known that same frustration: 'Bien entendu, l'ouvrier ignore l'usage de chaque pièce, 1] la manière dont elle se combine avec les autres, 2] la succession des opérations [. . .], 3] l'usage ultime de l'ensemble', *42,* p. 99.) Elise also notices Mustapha; and while at first believing herself to be greeting him 'machinalement' (p. 91/123), must soon accept that she has unknowingly ignored him for the past three days. If she has in fact been seeing her fellow-workers as machines it is because she has been little more than an automaton herself since starting at the factory. The exchange with Mustapha makes the point convincingly: the 'engourdissement dangeureux

[qui] détruisait tout effort de pensée' (p. 95/127) is dangerous precisely because one is unconscious of its approach.

Day 9 sees Elise feeling unwell and experiencing the inconvenience this causes; sick humans and broken machines are indistinguishable in that both create problems in the manufacturing process, and a set time is allowed for the 'repair' of each: Elise gets a quarter of an hour within which to recover. The image established from her first day of the factory as Hell – as quite literally godforsaken – is reinforced by means of one of Elise's understated observations: 'Autrefois, il y a quelques mois, était Dieu. Ici, je le cherche, c'est donc que je l'ai perdu' (p. 99/130). References to fire and flames here, which are linked to her newfound affection for her fellow-man, strike a note of defiance – is Elise challenging a God she has found wanting? – but again stress the connotations of Hell (as do the 'ronds de fumée' (p. 100/131) poisoning the atmosphere).

Day 11, the last to be selected for specific attention, sees Elise join the union, and the 'time-and-motion-studies man' observe the work rate. Elise notes that he does not time the workers' movements, but decides himself how rapid these ought to be, and draws up his plans accordingly. The parallel between worker and machine is forcibly underlined.

Having singled out certain events on particular days, Etcherelli allows the remaining weeks and months on the assembly-line to blur into each other for the reader as for Elise. Themes introduced earlier are returned to and developed in different ways. Thus the constant noise which initially so unnerved Elise is kept subtly to the forefront: the workers are repeatedly shown communicating by means of looks and gestures (it being hard to make oneself heard); the verbs 'appeler' and 'crier' replace 'dire' and 'répondre'; conversations are kept short; headaches are commonplace. Physical effects of the strenuous work are conveyed both by Elise's reference to her own exhaustion and her growing concern about Lucien's deteriorating health. Just how filthy the working conditions are is highlighted by the description of the new female workers (p. 134/160), and one constant reminder is the petrol-soaked rag Mustapha or Arezki regularly bring Elise – if this is filth that can only be removed with *petrol,* it is filth indeed. Small wonder that the glimpsed wall of the men's toilets bears the plea 'Des douches' (p. 163/185).

The psychological effects of the work and the working conditions are revealed via the major characters' impressions and in their conversations with other workers. For many, the light at the end of the tunnel is retirement; work, for those treated as mere instruments and denied any sense of self, is simply to be endured. 'L'usine, ça rend sauvages' (p. 102/133), says Arezki, ostensibly referring to the Arab immigrants, in fact describing the entire workforce. Lucien describes the effect on him in a speech to Henri (p. 137/162) which instantly and ironically recalls that earlier optimistic letter to Elise.

Etcherelli is in particular concerned to show how the very structures shaping the factory codes contrive to create discord: Arezki is refused permission to go to the infirmary because new Catch-22 regulations virtually state that any worker physically capable of reaching it cannot be in need of treatment; the work rate is stepped up because the person most qualified to judge a rhythm's acceptability, the foreman Gilles, is not consulted; work is deteriorating because no provision is made for training new workers; dissatisfaction is growing as experienced workers find their bonuses threatened by the incompetence of untrained novices. (Forfeiting bonuses for those with little money to spare is, as Elise quickly learns, a serious matter: 'Tant de gestes, si peu d'argent' (p. 123/150), she remarks when receiving her first wage-packet.)

Like Etcherelli herself, Lucien and Elise come to factory work as outsiders, fresh from the provinces and with a (comparatively) recently acquired political awareness which helped make 'la vraie vie' so very tempting. Outsiders see with fresh eyes but also have much to learn. Lucien sees the impossibility of writing impassioned articles after a day's work; Elise realises that not fraternity but fear rules in the factory. The war in Algeria and the racist tension complicate certain fears, create more, but have little to do with others. 'Le matin, l'angoisse de la journée à traverser . . . la peur de la pendule de pointage . . . la peur de ne pas aller assez vite . . . la peur de tous les menus accidents . . . la peur des engueulades' (*42,* p. 226). The list is Simone Weil's from a 1936 article; the fears, thirty years on, are the same. Discovering them at the same pace as Elise, testing them with a protagonist as new to factory life as is the average reader and seeing their effect on her, her brother and workmates, one is forced into an investigation of the various definitions of standards and qual-ity of living as proposed by the shapers of a modern industrial society dependent upon its manufacturing workforce – its proletariat.

4

L'usine au féminin

WRITING to an ex-pupil during the period spent working in various factories, Simone Weil explained that a male worker – provided that he be exceptionally skilful, intelligent and strong – might still hope eventually to work his way up to an interesting, worthwhile post (although with the development of 'rationalisation', this was becoming less and less of a possibility). But even so modest a hope was denied the women:

> Les femmes, elles, sont parquées dans un travail tout à fait machinal, où on ne demande que de la rapidité. Quand je dis machinal, ne croyez pas qu'on puisse rêver à autre chose en le faisant, encore moins réfléchir. Non, le tragique de cette situation, c'est que le travail est trop machinal pour offrir matière à la pensée, et que néanmoins il interdit toute autre pensée. Penser, c'est aller moins vite . . . (*42,* p. 32)

Some months after ending her experiment, she began a correspondence with the Managing Director of a factory, an engineer who had founded a workers' journal. Now able to look back on and evaluate her experience, Weil was eager that the (anonymous) engineer should learn from her findings, and in one letter, asked that he consider in particular her understanding of the position of the female worker:

> Autre remarque, que je mets par écrit pour que vous puissiez la méditer. En tant qu'ouvrière, j'étais dans une situation doublement inférieure, exposée à sentir ma dignité blessée non seulement par les chefs, mais aussi par les ouvriers, du fait que je suis une femme. (*42,* p. 202)

Some thirty years on, the glimpses Etcherelli was to give us into the world of the female factory worker would show how little had changed. Specifically emphasised is the toll the strenuous work takes on the women's health; conscious of how the young, apparently fit Elise suffers, we cannot but be aware of how older, more frail women must feel the strain even more keenly. A 1964 study, *Les Femmes O.S. dans la construction électrique,* paid particular attention to the effects both of the acceleration of work-rates and the repetitive nature of the women's tasks:

> Cette fatigue, que l'on nomme fatigue nerveuse, se traduit, d'après les propos recueillis parmi les ouvrières de l'électronique, des façons diverses, maux de tête, évanouissements, maux d'estomac, mauvaise humeur qui entraîne des conséquences au niveau familial (incapacité de supporter son mari et ses enfants), crises de nerfs, etc. . . . (*34,* p. 49)

It is this fatigue that becomes a way of life for Elise, this fatigue that persuades her female co-workers that all they have to look forward to is retirement – the day that for them, the machines, *la chaîne,* will stop.

'Si une femme travaille en usine, c'est vraiment qu'elle a des problèmes matériels épouvantables' (*3,* p. 27), Etcherelli stressed in the early Beauvoir interview. Most of the women she had herself worked with at the Citroën and SKV factories had been wives and mothers, to whom she paid tribute: 'Les difficultés que j'ai pu avoir n'étaient rien à côté de celles de ces femmes qui menaient une vie réellement inhumaine – ce dont, en général, leurs maris n'avaient pas l'air de se soucier beaucoup'.

Elise is in part concerned with exposing the particular difficulties facing the female factory worker, in many cases obliged to juggle such physically taxing work with the upkeep of a home and the various demands of family life. While comparatively little direct commentary is made on so stressful a situation, a few brief sketches suffice to bring out the difficulties it comprises – and the reader is of course constantly invited to compare Elise's own experience, and her reactions to it, with that of her female workmates.

The first part of the novel prepares the reader for those same reactions by showing the influences on Elise in those formative years of childhood and adolescence when her conception of woman's, and of her own, role was being shaped. Orphaned before adolescence, the teenage Elise's closest role-model of both mother- and womanhood is her grandmother, the poorly-educated cleaner whose homespun philosophising can be reduced to a few clichés, and all of whose energy goes into fighting off or denying poverty. Her own anxieties and frustrations are sublimated into housework: when Lucien is moody and insufferable his grandmother, not knowing what to say, *acts* instead – and scrubs out the cooker. The grandmother's influence, that of the nuns running the *patronage,* her schooling, the post-war press – a combination of all these elements make of the teenage Elise a true *Hausfrau* who keeps the house cosy and spotless, and who has a meal on the table for the homecoming male. (Anna is of course of the same generation, brought up mainly by women in a similarly impoverished environment. In her letter, which recounts amongst other things her first love-affair, she too reveals a similar early dream of blissful domesticity: 'Je rêvais d'une vie avec lui, de lui préparer un repas dans une cuisine fleurie' p. 36/78.)

With the introduction of Marie-Louise into the Letellier household Elise is obliged to make painful adjustments to accommodate 'l'étrangère détestée' (p. 24/68). No feeling of sisterhood is in evidence; indeed, when Marie-Louise becomes pregnant, Elise rejoices in what she sees as the deformed swollen body of her sister-in-law, and when Henri reappears and Marie-Louise is largely abandoned, Elise is triumphant: the intruder will now suffer the solitude she herself has had to endure.

But at this time Elise is beginning to read, beginning to understand more about world events and about herself: 'Je lisais et se levaient les voiles épais. [. . .] Je vis ma condition, j'en devins fière' (p. 25/69). Developing, this awareness gives new insights into the lives of others: thus, while continuing to resent her sister-in-law, Elise can no longer close her eyes to her heroic and uncomplaining efforts to straddle two worlds. At the biscuit factory, where she spends long hard hours on her feet, working with women whose men are also workers, Marie-Louise's life gradually becomes more difficult as workmates reject and ridicule new ideas she is acquiring from Lucien, and thus make it impossible for her to confide in erstwhile friends. At home, Lucien abandons his attempts to educate his wife 'au moment où son esprit [. . .] commençait à se délier' (p. 31/73). Marie-Louise is isolated: work over, she must return to look after her daughter and hope that Lucien will deign to come home. In desperation she turns for comfort to the advice columns and beauty pages of 'women's' magazines and to the grandmother, but remains unhappy in both spheres of her life, and is driven to emotional and physical exhaustion by the stress of trying to gain approval in both.

From resenting Marie-Louise, Elise comes to pity, and then, as Anna threatens to steal Lucien, almost to admire her. Henceforth many criticisms of Anna – of her artifice, of her manipulative nature, in particular of her laziness and pride – imply retrospective appreciation of Marie-Louise. This is an appreciation that the Elise 'narrating' from her Parisian hotel room underlines with one of the novel's rare acknowledgements of that true present from whose perspective events are viewed: '[Marie-Louise] était toute douce; *en ce temps-là,* je disais toute molle' (p. 33/75; my italics). Thus by the time Elise is preparing to return to Bordeaux, she may dread the notion of seeing the bereaved Marie-Louise – 'sa peine me fait injustement horreur' (p. 274/279) – but she has, largely because of her own working experience of the last nine months, learned to understand the particular pressures under which her sister-in-law had struggled.

It is of course by means of her own experience of work at the car-manufacturing factory that Elise and the reader learn about the life of those on the bottom rung of the ladder of participation in today's industrial society: the female factory worker in heavy industry.

Elise meets no women co-workers on her first day at the factory; what she does meet is the male workers' hostility to the new decision to employ women to inspect their work on the assembly-line. There is a general feeling that this is not women's work – not because it is dirty, physically demanding and potentially dangerous, but because women *aren't capable of grasping the essentials:*

> –Vous avez compris? demanda Daubat.
> –Un peu.
> –C'est pas un peu qu'il faut, dit-il en secouant la tête. Moi, je ne comprends pas pourquoi ils font faire ça par des femmes. (p. 80/114)

The implication is obvious: a man would have understood everything, instantly.

In workshop 76, Elise is initially the sole female worker; she only meets her women workmates in the cloakroom during breaks, and her natural reserve prevents her being easily accepted. She is therefore once again in the role of the outsider-observer. As someone for whom Marie-Louise's attempts at improving her appearance with make-up and accessories were essentially pitiful, she is for example very aware of what the use of such products in the factory signifies. In taking care to put on and regularly replenish lipstick and nail-varnish, the women are making a barely-conscious statement of defiance towards a job which in its monotony and dirtiness continuously militates against any desire to take pride in one's appearance – in one's self.

When the four new women workers are taken on to do tasks similar to that of Elise, the one who catches Elise's eye because of her resemblance to Marie-Louise is the one Mustapha finds prettiest, and also the one attracted to Lucien. Didi is young, brash, and has the self-confidence so alien to Elise. But although they have little in common, Elise has learned much over a short time, and is now able to appreciate characteristics she would previously have found puzzling (and did indeed find incomprehensible when they were exhibited by Marie-Louise). And so Didi's dressing in loud cheerful colours (in this greyest of places) to attract the men and that *need* to attract interest in an environment which persists in equating human beings with unresponsive machines – are phenomena Elise can now understand as the outward manifestations of an inner anger, an inner desire.

Certainly the somewhat cold and supercilious Elise of Part I is shown in Part II to have become considerably more responsive and sympathetic to her fellow-women. At the end of the day, as the workforce rushes to go home, she notices that those amongst the women who touch up their make-up ('neuf heures d'usine détruisaient le plus harmonieux des visages') are the young and single; the married women conserve their energy: 'Un autre travail les attendait, pour lequel il n'était pas nécessaire de s'embellir' (p. 155/178). As the Christmas break begins, Elise, who knows she will spend the holiday alone, is nevertheless not jealous of the departing women's high spirits: 'Elles payaient assez cher les plaisirs qui les attendaient' (p. 196-213), she notes. Learning more about their lives, seeing the toll the harsh work takes on the women, Elise cannot condone, but certainly understands, the motivation behind her cloakroom neighbour's 'Vivement la retraite' (p. 155/178). Wishing one's life away can hardly be blasphemous if that life is perceived as hardly ever being worth the living.

The women's racial prejudice, the changed attitude towards her once her relationship with Arezki is common knowledge, scares and repulses Elise, but she is aware that fear and ignorance have provoked this hostility – that it is the preconceived idea, and not the women themselves, that is responsible for the climate of hatred. Elise is now able to make such distinctions and to seek out motives behind such behaviour, having gained insight into the typical life of her women co-workers. Long-cherished ideas are shown up for the fabrications they are – thus, for example, the provincial myth of the capital and its highlife disintegrates as Elise realises that her fellow workers hardly ever leave their suburbs. Young women such as Didi still venture into the city, but most others remain within their own districts, penned in by poverty, or by the need to save money and thus to climb another rung of the socio-economic ladder as they perceive it: 'S'élever signifiait avoir, posséder. S'en sortir voulait dire acquérir. Des meubles, une voiture, en vingt ans un pavillon' (p. 224/237).

These are the values regulating the lives of Elise's female co-workers, the women whose lives are never-ending cycles of drudgery, treadmills they can only step off at retirement. The equating of a full and fulfilled life with the number of material possessions (objects) one amasses is hardly surprising in an environment where human worth is itself equated with a worker's ability to function like a machine (an object). And where that ability in a man is often, given the grading system of *P(rofessionnel)* and *O(uvrier) S(pécialisé),* more highly remunerated than in a woman kept at a lower grade (see *3,* p. 27), it is small wonder that the women themselves do not see their contribution as equal to that of the men – or indeed of much value at all. It is because of the denial of any sense of human dignity that such factory work typifies, rather than because of the physical weariness it induces, that the women seem prematurely aged and count the months and years until they retire.

In 1980 another young woman O.S., Dorothée Letessier, would write about a female factory worker who leaves work, husband and child to take a week off 'pour regarder sa propre vie de loin, fuguer' (*37,* p. 3). The tone, aim and scope of the novel bear little resemblance to *Elise*; the rare passages portraying the protagonist's normal working life do, however, echo Elise's own experience:

> Le corps se raidit à force d'être maltraité. Figés dans la position qui concilie le mieux la cadence et l'inconfort le plus supportable, nos muscles, nos nerfs se confondent avec la dureté de la matière et la vitesse des machines. Par moments, on ne sait plus si c'est la machine qui conduit le geste ou le geste qui conduit la machine. Tout baigne dans l'huile. On finit par ne plus comprendre d'où vient l'épuisement. (*37,* p. 15)

In the novels of both Letessier and Etcherelli, we are asked to consider what kind of a life this can be.

5

Structure, Style and Symmetry

'ELISE', John Roach has written, 'is deceptively simple, like a Lowry painting. But the apparent simplicity is carefully contrived' (*16,* p. 39). The remark holds good for the novel on several levels, that of its structure being no exception. Certainly the arresting opening paragraph, with its striking repeated negative infinitives, pulls us within barely forty lines back into the past of an anonymous female narrator; a temporary nine-line return to the present at the end of the first section excepted, it is in that past that we remain, a past recounted chronologically and which will, it seems safe to assume, meet up at some point with the narrator's present, and continue into her future. The novel may be composed of sections of varying lengths rather than of chapters but the flashback structure itself is strongly traditional; this, and the first-person narration, invite certain inevitable categorisations: a diary; an autobiography; personal reminiscences.

It is only on reading the last section, which definitively links the 'demain' of the first to 'le 22' of the antepenultimate, that it becomes apparent that the presenting of the events of the novel has been accomplished over a single night. It is this fact that has prompted Anne Ophir to point out that 'rien n'indique qu'Elise ait écrit son histoire', and to question: 'A-t-elle PENSÉ son histoire au fil du vécu? L'a-t-elle notée dans un journal?' (*15,* p. 215, note). Perhaps the question is unimportant; it affects the reader's role not one jot, and might lead to specious 'How-many-words-an-hour' arguments such as those that periodically rage around certain letter novels. But it does bring out an ambiguity which the apparently simplistic narrative technique belies; are we reading a testimony (Elise bearing witness because Lucien cannot?), or rather intruding on personal reflection?

The form of the novel – its two parts of unequal length, and their division into sections – means that either interpretation is tenable. In Part I, sections of relatively straightforward narrative recounting Elise and Lucien's upbringing are intermingled with those recounting moments of particular significance ('Le soir du réveillon . . .'; p. 17/62; the 1st March diary entry, p. 26/69), and others presenting people (Henri, p. 38/80; Anna, p. 48/88). These last are written in the narrative present, which has the effect of transforming paragraphs of written text into snapshots; it is as if, to illustrate her story, Elise has pulled out two old photographs (and indeed she notes of Anna that 'c'est une *image* banale qui est devant moi', p. 48/88; my stress). The rhythm of the novel is slowed down as these portraits are sketched; they hang in space as does the only other present-tense section in Part I, that which stresses the household's poverty, and the misplaced shame of the honest poor, described in the present because a constant, ever-present. Such sections contrast strongly with the final scenes of Part I, where the verbs of action piling up within a mere seven lines (p. 60/98) show Elise deciding to join Lucien, writing to him, warning employers of her imminent absence, cleaning the flat and preparing her clothes for the trip.

Part I constitutes approximately one fifth of the novel and is made up of some twenty sections; Part II, despite its length, comprises only forty-two. The sections are longer (and the time-period covered correspondingly shorter) for reasons set out on the first page, where we learn that the (then anonymous) narrator wants not to think, and particularly not to think about 'yesterday'. Describing childhood and adolescence has been a way of avoiding reference to the recent past; when the narrative brings us to Elise's arrival in Paris, however, it draws closer to the painful episodes of her story which she is reluctant to relive.

The sections are also on average longer because Elise is making discoveries: Paris, shabby hotels, the factory, and then her love for Arezki, his world, its dangers . . . such things are new and strange to her, and what is novel cannot be dismissed in a few lines (the first day at the factory alone requires some nineteen pages, the police raid on the Goutte d'Or flats nine). Once she has begun working at the factory Elise has little time for reflection, and the present tense is used sparingly and in short bursts which translate brief moments of self-consciousness: 'Je rêve à l'automne' (p. 98/130); 'Mon appétit est bon' (p. 106/136); 'Je vis ce jour [. . .] et je souffre' (p. 167/188). But as she gets used to the factory routine, Elise is able more easily to examine her surroundings and her workmates; thus bald accounts of procedures, of actions, give way to description and analysis.

It is a third of the way through the novel, on her ninth day at the factory, that Elise meets Arezki. Anne Ophir has stressed the sexual flavour of the very first description of him and his fiery glances, and of the effect he produces on Elise, who tries to neutralise it with the nurse's *tisane* (p. 103/134). Etcherelli builds up reader awareness of what is at this stage an unconscious attraction on Elise's part by having her draw our attention to the quality and speed of his work – and to the fact that they seem never to have a moment together. We are thus prepared for her to defy authority when Arezki is ill and is trying to gain permission to go to the infirmary – 'Le chef a dit non' (p. 124/151) – and for her to overcome shyness in order to offer her own aspirin. Henceforth the hesitant development of the Elise-Arezki relationship imposes its rhythm on the novel. Their first meeting outside the factory naturally prefigures a description of the women workers it would so shock (and an outing to Lucien's that Elise had significantly forgotten about). The second is followed by the romantic paean to nature, the ironic, euphoric passage which marks the definitive reawakening of Elise's sensuality, of those 'vieux rêves [. . .] enterrés, mais pas morts' (p. 143/168), and which, celebrating her own growing awareness, is at the centre of the novel. And from this point on, Elise's observations about the attitudes of her fellow Frenchmen towards Arab immigrants, Lucien's relationship with Anna, her own emotional development, etc., are as though sandwiched between the outings furtively arranged and discreetly embarked upon.

The last third of the novel can be said to begin in the midst of one of its longest sections with the discovery that Lucien has revealed the relationship to Bernier, and hence to the workforce in general. This lends an additional awkwardness but also an increased poignancy to Elise and Arezki's next meeting, underlined by the apostrophe 'Arezki, laisse tes cheveux s'égoutter . . .'

(p. 191/209). A certain acceleration now becomes evident. New event follows hard on new event; because what is no longer secret within the factory is so no longer outside it, Etcherelli can widen Elise's circle of acquaintances and thus validate her narrator's presentation of Arezki by showing him through different eyes. Elise is thus taken to see Arezki's uncle, his FLN comrades in Nanterre, his room. The police raid checks only momentarily what is for Elise an intensely active period; Arezki then takes her to a restaurant run by friends, and back to Nanterre; spring inspires the impromptu 'concert' in the factory; Lucien falls ill, and Elise reclaims his room.

But this last occurrence, the realisation of a long-cherished dream, in fact coincides with Arezki's surrendering of hope – 'Les rêves ne viennent plus' (p. 251/259) – and indeed, within a few days, he has lost his job. His growing despair has however been paralleled by Elise's optimism as the Europeans' uprising in Algiers seems to mark a turning point, and on 28th May comes the demonstration she invests with a significance exaggerated by desperation. But Lucien dies trying to participate in it and Arezki disappears. 'La vraie vie', remarks its narrator in the novel's penultimate section, 'aura duré neuf mois' (p. 274/279).

If we leave the novel conscious that this gestation period has in fact given birth to an individual whom we have watched grow to maturity and independence, this is in part because of the author's restrained but effective use of a 'flash-forward' device. We are never permitted to forget that this is a retrospective personal narrative. Infrequently but regularly Etcherelli causes her protagonist to recall her own (chronological) distance from the events recounted. A few pages into the novel Lucien is trying to interest Elise in a newspaper whose stand against the Indochinese war he approves; Elise, on hearing that it is condemning a distant war by which she cannot feel concerned, is utterly dismissive: 'Ah mais en Indochine!' (p. 21/65). In the face of this callous indifference, the older and wiser narrator is driven into revealing herself: 'Je me souviens de quel ton léger je lui dis cela'. The effect of this intervention is twofold: we are instantly reminded that the (more experienced) narrator is looking *back* on these events; and we are intrigued – what is going to happen (within the narrative; 'has happened' within the novel's real time scale) to make the light tone so . . . inappropriate? ironic? blameworthy? (Exactly why the narrator has singled out this incident is of course not yet apparent, and thus the desire to know how the tale develops – the suspense – is underlined and maintained.)

These interventions vary in form, and to a lesser degree in function. They comprehend examples of the 'Had I But Known' technique dear to Ogden Nash: 'cet automne-là [. . .] fut aussi, *mais je ne le savais pas,* le dernier avant que s'ébranlât [. . .] la charrette qui nous mènerait par des chemins détournés sur la pente où notre existence s'accélérerait' (p. 24/68); and again, 'cette crainte m'amena à une décision *qui devait changer tout mon avenir*' (p. 57/96; my stress). Such examples serve above all to enhance the element of suspense. Other such interventions include a reference to time and serve to keep the reader alert to the true 'now' of the narration: once in Paris, Elise can think more fondly of Marie-Louise, but '*en ce temps-là*' (p. 33/75) found her insipid; the letter she found from Anna was at the time read in secret, but '*aujourd'hui* je la possède à nouveau' (p. 35/77; my stress). Finally, the main purpose of a third group of such interventions is to reinforce our belief in the honesty and sincerity of the narrator. In these she takes herself to task directly by means of the rhetorical question – 'Pourquoi n'ai-je pas abandonné?' (p. 122/150) – or a moralising past conditional: 'J'aurais dû…' (p. 238/248; p. 256/264).

These last examples in particular contribute considerably to what Jean Gaugeard has termed 'l'authenticité' (*12*) of the novel, that honesty and a certain starkness that combine to make its hallmark. The use of the first person singular has many disadvantages which Etcherelli contrives skilfully to circumvent: the possible monotony of tone is counteracted by a variety of tempos and constant switches between conversational and more 'literary' styles; the single, often claustrophobic viewpoint is contrasted with the opinions of other characters; that same viewpoint is made to appear honest and genuine by its candid recounting of several incidents which show it in a bad light. But deft exploitation of that same first person brings its rewards, the major one being that an intimacy is established with the reader, who is obliged to assume that the narrator is speaking from lived – authentic – experience. When real events are interwoven into the narrative (as they are here by means of regular references to newspaper headlines) and the action occurs in actual locations, that authenticity is underlined, and that relationship of trust which must be established between the reader and the narrator reinforced. Etcherelli manipulates her chosen format with skill, allaying the apprehension that a first-person narration can breed, and maintaining the illusion that the reader and protagonist make their discoveries simultaneously, while periodically reminding us that the entire novel constitutes a flashback. As the 'je' that has begun relating itself one summer's evening returns us to the identical spot early the next day, we become aware not only that fewer than twenty-four hours have passed, but also that we can pinpoint those hours beginning at 7 p.m. on the night of Saturday, 21st June 1958. Such precision increases our sense of the text's authenticity – trusting the narrator, we have no need to check that this was indeed a Saturday – and it is surely not chance that Elise has, with customary modesty, chosen to tell her story on the shortest night of the year.

Etcherelli's use of language in *Elise* has been best analysed in an excellent article by Charles Camproux, in which he suggests that she has produced 'probablement l'exemple le plus achevé de ce que peut être le style réaliste' (*9,* p. 15). Camproux draws attention to her ear for the rhythms and vocabulary of popular speech; to the simple sentence structure 'vierge de toute recherche, même de la recherche de la simplicité' (*9,* p. 14); and to her use of tenses.

The question of tenses is an interesting one. The present of narration discussed above is of course used in contrast with the past historic traditionally used for past narration. This is the tense Etcherelli uses as a purist, making no attempt to avoid the heavy '-âmes' (etc.) endings of the first person plural, or the imperfect subjunctives tense-sequence requires but modern usage usually rejects. Such an approach means that the meditative nature of any passage in the present introduced into the main body of the text is accentuated much as is a monologue that comes between two conversations in a play (an example would be the intervention 'Ces pensées [. . .] dirait Lucien' (p. 166/188). Similarly, as Camproux underlines, the rare occasions on which the perfect tense is used see that tense demonstrating a function unique to it and indicating a succession of acts repeated over an unspecified time in the past – recollections of a love story are thus lent a rare intimacy, a sense of many shared moments combining to create one single experience:

> Arezki, lorsqu'il me rejoignit à Stalingrad, déclara que nous n'irions plus aux Ternes, ça n'était pas un bon quartier.
>
> –On va… au Trocadéro.
>
> Nous avons été au Trocadéro. Nous y sommes même revenus le surlendemain. Nous nous sommes promenés dans les jardins [. . .]
>
> Nous avons été à l'Opéra et fait plusieurs fois le tour de l'édifice.
>
> Nous avons traversé des ponts.
>
> Nous nous sommes perdus dans les rues du quartier Saint-Paul. . . (p. 181/200)

Another characteristic of Etcherelli's style in this novel is the comparative paucity of imagery. Her narrator's personality is such that she is particularly suspicious of attempts to enhance or colour: witness her mistrust of Anna, her repeated denigration of her own verbal proficiency. The very word 'image' suggests artifice to Elise and her own style is thus particularly denuded of simile and metaphor. The novel's first page shows her 'letting one by': 'Je veux partir sur un bateau qui ne fera jamais escale'; instantly, however, she disowns it as though ashamed – 'Cette image d'un bateau, je l'ai prise à mon frère'. Those she does use are usually hackneyed (and hence defused, their potency destroyed); the bonus is compared to the carrot dangled before a donkey, Elise's fixation with Lucien to a thorn that needs easing out.

That said, the banality of the images employed is subtly counter-balanced by comparisons (based on the four elements) which build towards the novel's final paragraph. The boat image is one of several references linking Lucien to water; the entry in his diary concerns the progress of a barge through water, Henri sees him as 'sans amarres' (p. 39/81) and calls him 'une épave' (p. 67/102). (Water would also appear to be the element of his mistress; Anna has '[des] cheveux de noyée, p. 49/89, and her face is 'comme une plage d'où la mer s'est retirée', p. 69/105.) Elise herself is linked rather to the earth; on the first page of the novel she sees a bedroom as 'une île flottante', and rather than compare the tale she is to relate to the progress of a meandering boat, uses the image of a cart jerking along the ground 'à petits tours de roues' (p. 24/68). Arezki is from his first appearance associated with fire, the 'feu noir allongé qui était son regard' (p. 100/131) accentuated in later references – 'ses yeux étincelaient [. . .] son regard s'éteignait' (p. 145/170). In the final paragraph of the novel, and only there, the four elements are united as Elise ponders over what she sees as several failures. From images of plants she moves on to that of a swollen tide, thence to ashes, and finally to the wind that will blow on and rekindle the fire of hope. The combining of the four elements creates a powerful image of wholeness, the wholeness Elise feels confident she can now achieve.

Just as that sparing use of imagery contributes to the 'apparent simplicity' stressed by Roach, so too does Etcherelli's selective use of qualifiers during sections where Elise is concerned primarily with recounting events. Contemplative parts of the novel, and those in which new characters or places are introduced, are naturally rich in emotive verbs and adjectives. But in those places where Elise, early established as a trustworthy observer where her brother is not concerned, slips into her role of witness, the would-be straightforward 'transcribing' of conversations, the relating of incidents, and the absence of direct comment, contrive to achieve an impression of objectivity. Etcherelli does not allow her character openly to judge or criticise in sections such as those recounting her first day at work, or her glimpse of the urinal wall; simply, we meet a Bernier who is 'impeccablement propre' (p. 77/111) and who shows Elise the assembly-line 'avec fierté' (p. 78/112); simply, we register that, of the comments carved into the wall, 'peu d'entre elles étaient obscènes' (p. 163/185). The points are made unobtrusively, but made they are.

Equally subtle is Etcherelli's exploitation of the values of various pronouns. The division of the factory-work experience into specific numbered days before they merge into a routine is important to the plot – significant events mark each of the differentiated days – and to the establishing of a work rhythm to which both Elise and the reader are slowly to become accustomed. And that gradual process of assimilation is indicated by the play of pronouns. Day 1, where everything is new and impressions need recording, is of course dominated by the 'je': 'j'aurais voulu qu'il m'expliquât ce qui se passait avant que la voiture arrivât jusqu'à moi' (p. 86/119). By Day 4, the next day singled out, Elise is beginning to differentiate between her workmates; her request is repeated, but the change in pronoun mirrors her change in attitude: 'Si on voyait par où passe la voiture, d'où elle vient, où elle va, on pourrait s'intéresser, prendre conscience du sens de ses efforts' (p. 94/126). The collective but impersonal 'on' itself makes way on Day 9 for the 'nous' of solidarity – 'Attachés à nos places' (p. 98/129), 'Rivés à la chaîne comme des outils. Outils nous-mêmes' (p. 108/137) – and, because this day marks the introduction of Arezki, a second 'nous' makes its appearance as Elise notices the newcomer, with whom she has less contact than she would like: 'Nous ne nous trouvâmes jamais ensemble' (p. 105/135). Finally Days 11 and 12 accentuate the distancing third person reserved for the managerial staff: Lucien advises Elise to cultivate a certain insolence: 'Les chefs sont des aboyeurs. Ne leur ôte pas ce plaisir' (p. 120/148). Gilles deplores 'their' imposing extra duties on workers already over-stretched: 'C'est trop [. . .] Je le leur ai fait observer' (p. 122/149). The progression of pronouns effectively parallels and accentuates Elise's gradual immersion and involvement in factory life.

There is a certain thematic symmetry in this novel, in that the theme of a young female factory worker, who is ostracised by co-workers for loving a man of whom they disapprove, could be said to be introduced by means of the Marie-Louise/Lucien couple and taken up, greatly amplified, as Elise goes on to recount her own experience. A similar kind of symmetry, a pairing of linguistic echoes, creates various linkings on the level of language which serve to stress several major issues.

Etcherelli bestows upon her narrator a sensitivity to and respect for words which is early established and repeatedly underlined: 'Je cherchai mes mots', we read of Elise a few pages into the novel. 'Je voulais être adroite' (p. 22/66). She modestly deplores the difficulty she has in expressing herself – ('Je cherche, sans trouver, comment décrire . . .', p. 195/212); and regularly draws attention to her own interest in words by commenting on how others (Lucien, p. 66/102, Arezki, p. 197/214) manipulate them. It is she who invests Arezki's use of the name Hawa with such mystique by refusing to ask what it means; she, in short, who establishes various terms as particularly significant – 'la vraie vie' being a case in point – so that the reader comes to recognise them as verbal signposts guiding him throughout the novel.

Thus primed, we are receptive to the way Elise's exhausted 'Je me laverai tout à l'heure' (p. 90/122) echoes, or retrospectively stresses, Lucien's 'Je me laverai demain' (p. 66/101). Daubat's dismissive 'Vous croyez que ce sont des hommes?' (p. 86/119) serves to prefigure the policeman's disdain during the Goutte d'Or raid: 'Tu appelles ça des femmes! ' (p. 218/232). Lucien's explanation of the immigrants' wolf-whistling – 'A travailler comme ça, on retourne à l'état animal' (p. 83/116) – is reformulated by Arezki: 'L'usine, ça rend sauvages' (p. 102/133). Such reinforcement ensures that the single voice of the narrator, or its single viewpoint, is backed up by one or more of the other characters on matters where a glimpse of other opinions confirms us in the one we are ourselves formulating. There is even numerical echoing: the number of the workshop coincides with that of the article under which Arezki may be held or expelled: 'atteinte à la sûreté intérieure et extérieure' (p. 269/275); Lucien's age at his death is reproduced in the date his sister chooses to leave Paris . . .

It is possible to take the interest generated by the name Hawa, revealed at the end of the book as meaning Eve, as an invitation to look more closely than is perhaps usual at the proper names in this novel – an invitation stressed by the doctor's generalising 'Tous les Arabes s'appellent Mohammed' (p. 75/110); predictably, we never meet one. If Lucien is the 'light' that Elise, 'consecrated to God', follows to Paris (where she meets her counterpart 'Gift from God' Arezki), he is also the husband of the understandably 'bitter battle-maid', the lover of Anna 'full of grace', chooses to name the daughter of a disappointing union 'bitterness', and has as his closest friend the middle-class Henri (significantly 'ruler of the estate' or 'lord of the manor'). And what of the appropriateness of the names of the elder from Arezki's village (Si Hacène, 'the good man'), and of the devoted communist Gilles ('a shieldbearer')?

Finally the novel contains an example of verbal ricochet which threads throughout Part II to give valuable insight into a matter dear to Elise's heart – and to that of her creator. Prior to leaving for Paris, Elise is finding that living alone is less difficult than she had thought: 'La solitude du soir n'était pas douloureuse. Je me sentais en sécurité chez moi. Sécurité. J'aimais ce mot et ce qu'il évoquait. J'en aimais la sonorité rude. Sécurité' (p. 58/97). Thus far the repetition has underlined the importance of a feeling of security for Elise. But she continues: 'Il commençait comme serrure. Il remplaçait le mot bonheur'.

The notion of security 'replacing' happiness invests the word with such a weight of significance that the preceding phrase can easily slip by unchallenged, and the reader retains an image of security (and) locks – ('serrure de surêté') – of the price of security being freedom, etc. Indeed this is the image we are meant to retain – despite the fact that all the two words have in common is the initial [se] ([sɛ] also being a possibility for 'serrure'), which is something they share with several hundred other words. It is a measure of how central this image is felt to be that this weakest of similarities is so stressed…

Thus sensitised, the reader next registers that Didi, the new worker, 'contrôle les serrures' (p. 129/156). Will this mean that she will similarly influence Elise's happiness, her security? Certainly Elise will later find her 'Allah, Allah!' most hurtful. And when, in the meantime, Arezki and Elise's first meetings lead them to walk along the boulevard 'Serrurier', the fragility of the happiness, of the momentary security they will find together, is brought forcibly to our attention.

Interestingly, however, there is no boulevard Serrurier in Paris; the boulevard of which Elise is thinking at the Porte des Lilas is named after an eighteenth century Count Sérurier. The misspelling would seem, like the tenuous 'serrure-sécurité' link, to underline the importance of the notion of security to both Elise, and her creator. It is finally perhaps worth recording that into the boulevard Sérurier, with all its accumulated connotations of safety in imprisonment, runs . . . the boulevard d'Algérie.

6

Threads

CERTAIN leitmotifs weave their way through *Elise,* some making a brief appearance now and then when a particular effect of emphasis is required, others, more obvious, looping through the novel like a seamstress's tacking stitches (and performing a similar function). Anne Ophir has, for example, stressed the importance of *le regard*; John Roach has highlighted the repeated evocation of the police presence. Both naturally also accentuate 'la vraie vie'. While the latter must demand our initial attention, and while the other threads referred to are similarly worthy of note, others such as the Journey, *la Chambre* and the Weighting of Words also merit exploration.

LA VRAIE VIE

Claire Etcherelli has expressed a liking for 'les titres à plusieurs facettes' (*18*), and that of her first novel is certainly satisfyingly enigmatic. The expression 'la vraie vie' doubtless comes, as several critics have suggested, from Rimbaud's *Une saison en enfer*; it is of interest to note that the poet is talking of a lack, of a negative entity: 'Quelle vie! La vraie vie est absente'. And the adjective 'vrai' is in itself interesting, having several meanings, and, equally, being able to temper the significance of these according to its position with relation to the substantive. In short, the title simultaneously conjures up images of what is perhaps best rendered in English as Life in the Real World (a phenomenon schoolchildren and students are frequently enjoined to await with trepidation, which stands in opposition to any way of life judged too lax or too cloistered), and of a serenely happy life achieved thanks to the fulfilment of a nebulous ideal, and which fuels hope for the future. Etcherelli is concerned not to pin down the phrase, which is several times echoed by the main characters, and which is invested with various levels of significance according to which character employs it.

The young Elise met in the first few pages of the book, revelling in the dull existence she has chosen because she can control it, feels no need to seek another life; she is content with, and refuses to look beyond, what she terms 'la vie droite' (p. 12/57), which she has itemised, its distinguishable components comprising 'une table prête, une maison rangée, des visages tranquilles' (p. 12/57). When Lucien's bad temper and threats become a strain, it is from the notion of creating 'une petite vie à moi' (p. 20/64) that Elise derives most comfort; as she rearranges her belongings 'tout rentrait dans l'ordre, dans mon ordre' (p. 20/64). Indeed her brother is careful to reflect her own ideal back at her when seeking her support for his marriage: 'La vraie vie', he tells her, 'c'est comme toi. Le calme, la paix en dedans. [. . .] Crois-moi, Elise, je suis pressé d'être marié pour atteindre cette vie-là' (p. 22/66). For her part, Elise understands his strategy, but also sees how it works, knowing herself transparently vulnerable to images of 'la vie tranquille, droite, simple' (p. 22/66).

It is then not to Elise but to Lucien that it first falls to echo the title. At this juncture, in love for the first time, eager to begin married life, Lucien sees 'la vraie vie' as essentially calm and serene. Barely a year later, his wife and child mere burdens, his discussions with Henri his only real activity, he is preparing to seek it elsewhere: it is now a dream, an ideal. And Elise begins to align her aims with his:

> Lucien soupirait parfois quand il était avec son ami:
>
> –Un jour, ce sera la vraie vie, on fera tout ce qu'on veut faire.
>
> On fera tout ce qu'on veut faire. Lucien affirmait. Oui, nous réaliserions nos rêves, nous irions rejoindre ceux qui vibraient comme nous. (p. 33/75)

From this point in the novel until brother and sister are working in the factory, 'la vraie vie' is used to signify an idealised existence, a permanent 'one day', a dream not to be analysed.

Lucien has embarked upon a new, tortuous but stimulating relationship and is also, thanks to Henri's letters from Paris, projected into the heady climate of the capital; 'la vraie vie' has thus become that which awaits him if he can just slough off the old (married, provincial) life: 'Tu verras, un jour commencera la vraie vie. [. . .] Le principal, c'est d'y arriver intact' (p. 49/89). Elise, still blinking after emerging from behind the 'voiles épais' (p. 25/69) her reading has parted, is now brimming over with questions: What exactly was 'la vraie vie'? 'Qu'est-ce que cela changerait? A quoi saurait-on que la vraie vie commençait?' (p. 49/89).

The expression thus corresponds above all to an adventure into the unknown, and Elise both yearns for and fears it. At the moment of Lucien's departure for Paris, panic wells up in the sister who has never before been parted from him; in her desperation and loneliness she is willing to abandon all dreams, to settle for what she has and knows: 'Il jouait à partir, il allait défaire sa valise, je ne pouvais rester seule. Tant pis pour la vraie vie. Et qui sait si elle n'était pas ici dans les longues rêveries, dans l'attente et le désir d'ailleurs?' (p. 56/95). But the invitation to join Lucien dispels apprehension. In accepting it Elise, heading north on 'le train de la revanche' (p. 60/98), is both taking her revenge on her grey, cheerless past and acknowledging her own quest for 'la vraie vie'.

If in Part I the phrase refers almost exclusively to an ill-defined ideal, Part II confronts the idealised with the inescapably real. In a very early review of the novel André Dalmas stressed that what Elise must come to terms with 'ne sera pas le mirage de la vie rêvée, mais la vie véritable' (*10*); writing three years later about Michel Drach's film, Jean-Louis Bory would distinguish between 'la vraie vie, celle que l'on rêve de mener', and 'la vie vraie, celle que l'on mène' (*23*). Manipulated into taking a job at the factory, Elise senses that something of significance is about to take place: '"Ça commence", me dis-je, sans pouvoir définir ce qui commençait' (p. 71/106). She is of course about to come face to face with 'la vie vraie' – prosaic, numbing, dream-shattering, and hardly what she has travelled to Paris to experience.

By her ninth day at the factory, Elise has begun to express in her own terms that 'vie vraie/vraie vie' dichotomy. She savours each minute of her bus journey: 'J'avais cinquante minutes d'irréalité. [. . .] Pendant cinquante minutes, je me dérobais. La vraie vie, mon frère, je te retiens! Cinquante minutes de douceur qui n'est que rêve' (p. 98/129). There is a hint of bitterness in the wry shrug (Well, brother, so this is your famous 'vraie vie'); the paradoxical opposition between 'la vie réelle' and an ideal 'vraie vie' is never so keenly felt, the distance between the two, of which Bory speaks, never so pronounced.

But with the very next page Etcherelli introduces the one 'instrument' capable of enabling Elise to reconcile 'vie vraie' and 'vraie vie'. As Arezki's and Elise's relationship develops, as reactions in the factory and on the street sensitise Elise to anti-Algerian feeling, it becomes clear that life is moving too fast to permit reflections on its essential nature. Eventually, however, Elise feels the need to take a lunchtime walk; the rêverie it gives rise to constitutes one of the novel's rare passages of lyricism, and reveals Elise's need to weigh up her experience to date. Passing recent events in review, she moves towards an understanding of life, of 'la vraie vie', as a synthesis of not necessarily quantifiable elements:

> Ces pensées, le froid, les mèches qui volent dans mon cou, la dérobade d'Arezki, le sang du Magyar et l'odeur de l'usine, les quatre heures de chaîne qui m'attendent, la lettre de la grand-mère que je n'ai pas encore lue, c'est tout cet amalgame, la vie. Comme elle était douce, celle d'avant, la vie un peu floue, loin de la vérité sordide. Elle était simple, animale, riche en imaginations. Je disais 'un jour…' et cela me suffisait.
>
> Je vis ce jour, je vis la vraie vie, mêlée aux autres humains, et je souffre. (pp. 166-67/188)

What Elise has learned is that 'la vraie vie' is not a definable entity but rather an attitude, a state of mind. Any life – any kind of life, anybody's life – merits the qualifier provided that it can be perceived, even if only by its 'owner', as being *significant,* and making some kind of mark. If Elise herself is living a 'vraie vie' it is because Arezki, leading figure in both her real and her ideal lives, has illustrated the possibility of successfully blending the two. He literally makes sense of her life – 'ma vie avait trouvé un sens' (p. 207/223). Elise can now recognise this, and that recognition, in turn, is a vital part of Elise's education ('La vraie vie', Etcherelli would underline in a 1977 interview, 'c'est la prise de conscience'; *16,* p. 39).

With the death of her brother and the disappearance of Arezki Elise hands in her notice and prepares to return to Bordeaux, 'la vraie vie', as she flatly comments, having lasted nine months. It is however plain that Elise will not be able to sink back into what she once so damningly dismissed as a life 'que l'on regarde passer' (p. 224/237). Once initiated, one is indelibly marked by 'la vraie vie'; it fosters hope, it leaves scars. Elise cannot withdraw from it; after a necessary period of mourning, of lying fallow, she must inevitably rejoin it.

The journey

The theme of the journey is one that is closely linked to that of 'la vraie vie'. Initially, although the then anonymous narrator borrows the image, the notion of travelling is firmly linked to Lucien: 'Je n'aime pas les aventures. Je veux partir sur un bateau qui ne fera jamais escale. Embarquer, débarquer, cela n'est pas pour moi. Cette image d'un bateau, je l'ai prise à mon frère, Lucien' (p. 9/55). The impression is given that the narrator, not liking 'aventures', has avoided them; only gradually will it become clear that she has of late encountered too many for her peace of mind.

Lucien, then, is presented as the traveller – but to travel is not always to develop, to broaden the mind. As a child, Lucien often goes to watch the boats, seemingly eager to undertake his own voyage of discovery; and of course he finally decides that only by travelling to Paris will he experience 'la vraie vie'. But although Lucien may always seem to be on the move, going to meetings, to Paris, and is indeed killed literally on the road, he seems to learn little on his travels. He may lose some simplistic theories about immigrant/French worker solidarity, but there is no evidence that a maturing process is at work. In essence, he and Anna are dabblers; mesmerised by ideology, forever picking up books on various subjects, they then discard them as a new interest presents itself. Lucien also makes no progress in understanding those he has ostensibly come to Paris to champion; if he had any notion of how the FLN functioned, he would not have put Arezki in danger by making public his relationship with Elise.

Elise herself is not usually a devotee of images of boats travelling ever onwards. Reflecting her more down-to-earth nature, she gives but one image of travel: that of a cart lurching along as does her life, clumsily, and taking many detours. And yet it is she who makes the longest and the most complete voyage of discovery – of self-discovery. As she writes her account she is also making a journey into time, one which covers over two decades but which in fact, as we realise at the close of the novel, has in the 'true' time of the narrative, taken only one night. And that account is an account of a journey: from child to adult, girlhood to womanhood, as well as from Bordeaux to Paris.

Within that major journey are several smaller ones. It can be very instructive to readers less familiar with Paris to trace Elise's outings on a map, for Elise explores Paris as she explores the new life it offers. We are never told how she spends the first few weeks; any journeys around the capital she may have made then are thus unimportant. But from the moment she begins work, her journeys are charted in detail; and whereas Bordeaux was never named, and few of its features were described, areas and routes in Paris are dwelt upon – 'la vraie vie' happens in a 'vraie ville' with 'vraies rues'. Thus the first journey described – from the northern Porte de la Chapelle to the Porte de Choisy – is detailed not only to reinforce the idea that Elise is in the capital, but also shows every reader who knows Paris that she is living in one working-class district, and having to travel to the other side of the city to work in another.

On the one occasion Elise is invited to accompany Lucien to a meeting, they penetrate only a little way into the city: if the capital itself and 'la vraie vie' in any way parallel each other, it becomes clear that it is not with her brother that Elise will explore them. But the relationship with Arezki is built upon short journeys, and their every walk is thus doubly a progression. Their first and second outings take them to the north-eastern limits of Paris; they then penetrate to the district Elise visited with her brother and Anna; and subsequent walks take them into the centre of Paris – to the Trocadéro and the rue de Rivoli. Like the young Rastignac of *Le Père Goriot,* Elise learns much from these sorties: police round-ups, the lights of the Champs-Elysées, the tower blocks of Nanterre, all are explored and recorded. If Paris can be seen as a symbol, for Elise, of 'la vraie vie', it is only with Arezki that she goes to the heart of it.

The closing pages of the novel trace another journey, from Mantes and Lucien's funeral back to Paris. On reaching the capital, Henri suggests they take the main ring road to get to the northern area in which Elise lives: once again she is restricted to the outer limits of Paris, and indeed will shortly abandon the city completely as 'la vraie vie' has abandoned her. At first, passing the Cité Universitaire, she is hopeful. The university buildings seem to symbolise civilisation for her: 'à cause [. . .] des vieilles pierres et de quelques étudiants qui gagnent le boulevard, je me dis qu'Arezki ne risque rien' (p. 269/275). Just past these halls of residence, she tries to rationalise her fears: 'Il y a les avocats, les journaux. La vie d'un homme, elle a du poids ici' (p. 269/275). But as they pass her old place of work, despair sets in. Crossing over the Seine she thinks of the bodies – and how many of them Algerian? – that have been, and will be, thrown off that bridge into it. And hope dies: 'La vie d'un Arabe est de quel prix ici?' They drive quickly towards Pantin, the boulevard paralleling the boulevard de Sérurier, and then enter the tunnel under the Porte de la Villette: 'Je pressens que je ne verrai plus jamais Arezki' (p. 271/277). What Paris gave, Paris has taken away. We leave Elise prior to her return journey to Bordeaux, which will complete the circle in space that mirrors the novel's 'circle in time'.

La chambre

When her third novel appeared in 1978, Claire Etcherelli was interviewed for *La Quinzaine littéraire.* In reply to Anne Manceron's observation that the room was obviously a very important issue for her, she concurred: 'la chambre [. . .] sert toujours de révélateur. C'est à partir de la chambre que quelque chose éclate, se déploie' (*18*). Rented rooms do indeed play a major role in *Elise:* they are of course revealing of character, but it is their function as refuge and as incubator that is perhaps most striking.

Chronologically, the first room of significance is the bedroom Elise occupies, in the family's two-bedroom flat, until she is fifteen. It is used as currency: she offers it to Lucien 'pour le gagner à moi' (p. 10/56), but soon regrets the gesture when he begins to shut himself away in it. When he breaks his leg he hibernates in it, reading, thinking, following the war on his wall-map. It has become an incubator; within it, Lucien is growing, and from it, he first glimpses Marie-Louise.

This is the room that Elise is several times driven to search. Rifling through her brother's things, she is not looking for anything specific; simply, she is fighting to understand Lucien, and is seeking answers to her questions in the contents of his cupboards. The day he marries, Elise spends the night in his room, 'avec le sentiment d'étreindre quelque chose qui allait définitivement m'échapper' (p. 23/67). It is an effort to stay close to him.

Etcherelli has said that things 'burst out' of 'la chambre', so many plans and schemes being hatched from within its walls. Once the novelty of married life wears off, Lucien shuts himself away with the newly-returned Henri; animated discussions in the little room go on far into the night, discussion that will eventually inspire Lucien to go to Paris. When Henri leaves for the capital, Lucien shuts himself away in the room to reply to his friend's letters; it has become a sanctuary which one can only enter if invited. For Elise it is finally profaned when, Marie-Louise convalescing, Lucien invites Anna to stay. The disgust

Elise feels when she hears her brother and Anna arguing has nothing to do with any consideration for his wife; Elise's reaction is shown to spring from her sense that the flat has been defiled, *because* it has been taken over: 'Un brusque dégoût s'empara de moi. Ils s'installaient partout' (p. 54/93).

When she arrives in Paris Elise initially has no strong feelings about the various rented rooms she inhabits (although she resents the fact that her last move is occasioned by the reappearance of Anna). The affection for the room in Bordeaux lingers; later, when it seems to her that Arezki has lost interest in her, she consoles herself with the thought that she will soon be returning home, and will be able to take over and rearrange her old room: 'Ce sera la mienne et je l'arrangerai à ma guise' (p. 153/176). On those four walls at least, Elise knows she can impose her personality.

As her friendship with Arezki grows, the fact that the couple has nowhere to go to avoid the hostility encountered in the streets becomes a central issue. Arezki is the first to articulate the feeling of constraint and frustration, and although his strength of feeling ostensibly alarms Elise, she cannot help but imagine, during their visit to Arezki's uncle, how she could clean and brighten up the little garret. Elise is both pleased and apprehensive when Arezki repeats the need for a room. (It is noticeable that it is not the privacy, but the shelter, that is uppermost in his mind: 'tu m'attendrais à l'abri', p. 206/222.) Wanting this, Elise is simultaneously unable to bring herself actively to seek it; this inability fully to lay to rest the various *idées reçues* from her past is presented as a permanent, insoluble problem. Arezki's own shared room in the notorious Goutte d'Or district becomes the only possibility; it is this room, with the new bedspread bought especially for Elise's first visit, that becomes the scene of the intimidating police raid, which numbs Elise and silences Arezki for three days.

Because of their failure to obtain use of the uncle's room, and after the marking experience of the raid that defiled Arezki's own lodgings, the fact that Lucien's illness frees for a while the room he has shared with Anna is seen as '[un] miracle' (p. 244/254). Although still haunted, in Elise's eyes, by her brother and Anna, this becomes her and Arezki's room, where, despite the disapproval of the hotel manager, they are able to snatch a few hours together. But the shelter it affords is not theirs for long – Arezki disappears, 'la chambre' (p. 260/267) being the last words he utters. His and Elise's sanctuary, once that of Anna and Lucien, will become that of Anna and Henri. 'La vraie vie', in which this room has played an important part, ends for Elise as she leaves it.

WORDS: (I) THE WRITTEN WORD

Etcherelli's early belief in the power of the written word, which would lead to her becoming a novelist, is evident from her explanation of why she has, for a long time, kept a diary: 'Résolution d'adolescente austère qui croyait à la qualité, au pouvoir de l'écrit, qui le considérait comme une grille capable de déchiffrer sa propre complexité, celle du monde' (*17*). That belief is something she transmits to Elise; it becomes a characteristic of her protagonist, an important element in her process of self-discovery.

The first mention of the impact the written word can have upon Elise is dramatic. Elise is effecting her own education by delving into Lucien's books and magazines, and this crucial contact with the written word is a liberating experience: 'Je lisais et se levaient les voiles épais' (p. 25/69). The sensual pleasure the very act of reading procures is emphasised, together with the intellectual gain of taking in new information and ideas: 'C'était une impression pareille à la musique. Me délier, comprendre, pénétrer au milieu des mots, suivre la phrase et sa logique, savoir. Je ressentais une satisfaction physique' (p. 25/69).

Worshipping the written word, Elise attaches great importance to Lucien's personal diary. When she cannot understand his behaviour – when oral communication between them breaks down – she invades his room and his privacy to find it, seeking clues to his behaviour; the brother who she senses is so distant may be encapsulated in his diary. On one occasion she discovers the letter from Anna lying between its pages. (It is of interest to note that we learn by means of a 'flash-forward' (p. 35/77) that Elise has it in her possession at the close of the novel; she cannot lightly throw away a written, personal testimony such as this.) This discovery, in Elise's own scheme of things, marks the end of an era; not because it is proof that Lucien is 'straying', since this is known already, but rather because this is the only *written* evidence. As a written declaration of love, the letter is something almost holy for Elise; it has a finality to which she is all too sensitive.

The example of the written word to which attention is most frequently drawn is that of the newspaper headline. Before going to Paris, Elise savours what she sees as the 'formule magique' (p. 46/87) of those headlines – magical, because of their power to conjure up exotic worlds and cultures. Once in the capital, she is at first intrigued by them in much the same way: 'On demandait des mesures exceptionnelles' (p. 90/123), she learns, and instantly begins to suspect her fellow bus passengers of belonging to the FLN. But gradually she grows instead to fear them and their power, as she begins in part to understand Arezki's involvement in the movement. The headlines are periodically brought into the narrative – 'Réseau FLN démantelé à Paris' (p. 159/182) – to reinforce awareness of the contemporary climate, just as street names impress upon the reader the fact that events are taking place in known areas of a real city.

Even in the factory, instances where the written word serves to make a point are not lacking, and each arouses the interest of Elise. Mustapha's sign 'NE TU SE PAS' is what attracts Elise's attention to him; this written message, once deciphered, is what causes her to feel 'un élan de sympathie' (p. 95/126), is what gives rise to the interest she feels in her young fellow worker. The graffiti she glimpses in the men's toilet are also recorded; the moving 'Vive la Légeri' and the practical demand for 'Nos cinq francs' (p. 163/185) say more about the preoccupation of the workforce than might several expository paragraphs. Elise hoards such moments, such pieces of evidence, collecting them like stamps. It comes as no surprise to learn that she enjoys crosswords; words and their power – to incite to action, to destroy – are of paramount importance to her. And she also knows how sensitive she is to them; their attraction lies in their capacity to liberate, to evoke potent images which set her dreaming. When the word 'blé' presents itself to her as the answer to one of the clues, it induces rêverie: 'l'image resta, avec ses couleurs, sa sinuosité gracieuse, évocatrice de fraîcheur et d'espace' (p. 212/227).

Given the attraction the written word holds for her, and the pattern that begins with Lucien's books, his magazines, and includes his diary and his lover's letter, it is somehow fitting that Elise should learn of her brother's death . . . in the columns of a newspaper.

(II) Personal vocabularies

Elise's sensitivity to the written word goes hand in hand with a wary respect for the spoken. She takes pleasure in words and their sounds – the linking of 'sécurité' and 'serrure' is a case in point – but also handles them with the greatest care, repeatedly bemoaning an imagined awkwardness in using them. Thus when Bernier begins to find fault with Elise's work because he has learned of her relationship with Arezki, she is at pains to stress a weakness which she feels limits her ability to cope: 'Je n'avais ni le vocabulaire ni l'assurance nécessaires pour lui tenir tête' (p. 206/221). (Indeed, this real or apparent lack is of great significance; more confidence in her ability to manipulate words might have allowed Elise to settle the later disagreement with Bernier herself, rather than losing her control and throwing down her clipboard to attract Arezki's attention.)

When Elise begins work at the factory, the vocabulary particular to the car-body is new to her. Amongst all the other things she is learning, Elise finds the time to comment on and record terms which are novel to her: putting a completed inspection sheet on the shelf under the rear windscreen she notes that 'on disait plage [arrière], je venais de l'apprendre' (p. 81/115). There is a sense in which words are the key to this new job for Elise: understand the vocabulary – crack the code – and the puzzle is solved.

Other people's use of words – their own personal vocabularies – tend to form yardsticks for Elise: one of the ways she judges others is by the terms and expressions they habitually employ. When she first joins Lucien in Paris, what strikes her just as much as his much weakened physical condition is his new, more brusque way of expressing himself – his choice of words: 'Il s'exprimait avec une grande économie [. . .]: "roule, amène, en piste, file, d'accord, je me casse, salut, attige" et quelques mots obscènes fraîchement appris' (p. 66/102). It is similarly by means of his choice of phrasing, to which his sister's ears are perfectly attuned, that Lucien reveals that he is about to ask a favour: Elise senses this, and experiences 'un mauvais pressentiment' because 'il usa de précautions oratoires à mon intention' (p. 66/102).

Given her sensitivity to words it is not surprising that, on first meeting the Hungarian worker, she is struck by the loneliness he must feel because he does not speak French: 'Il ne parlait pas le français et travaillait sans un mot [. . .] A imaginer la solitude de cet être sans contact avec rien [. . .] je me jugeais privilégiée' (p. 105/135). Nor that, overhearing the women's comments on those known to 'fraternise' with the Algerian workers, she immediately reacts to the image they evoke: '"elle marche avec les Algériens". Ces mots évoquaient des bouges tristes où la même femme passe successivement dans les bras de beaucoup d'hommes' (p. 174/194).

And it is fitting that the man with whom she falls in love, and to whose use of language she is therefore most sensitive, should also be extremely wary of words and their power. Elise notes that 'Arezki pardonne difficilement. "Je te jure" et "ma parole" coupent dix fois ses phrases. Il aime le mot "frère", et il dit "notre peuple". D'ailleurs, c'est avec prudence qu'il choisit ses mots, comme s'il leur conférait un pouvoir' (p. 197/214). Like Elise, he has no confidence in his powers of expression. Trying to explain why Mustapha should not allow racist remarks to affect him, he feels unequal to the task: 'Tu demanderas à ton frère de t'expliquer, il le fera mieux que moi; il me manque les mots justes' (p. 209/224). Attempting to give reasons for wanting a shirt that would cost a week's pay, a shirt that would shock worn by an Algerian factory-worker, he feels that his explanation would not be accurate, and voices that frustration: 'Si je pouvais t'expliquer ça avec des mots pour me faire comprendre' (p. 193/210).

Yet despite a lack of confidence when trying to express complex reactions, Arezki takes pleasure in punning, in creating with words, deforming 'le square de la Limagne' ('Arezki disait "de la Limace"'), creating a 'Mont de Pitié' ('j'aimais beaucoup ce dernier mot', p. 270/276), and, of course, baptising Elise 'Hawa'. Not being able to translate the term does, of course, give it an air of mystery, lends it charm, to an Elise so sensitive to words, and her lover's use of them.

The ultimate power that can be accorded to words is that of telling a life – of recounting that life's truths. Whether or not we see this novel as a recording of the thoughts of that last night in Paris, or as a written testimony of Elise's experiences, the fact remains that she has entrusted her tale to her own mastery of the word, aware of its limitations, aware also that she has taken over the role of witness Lucien could not fulfil, and endeavoured to speak out for those who could not do so themselves.

7

Bildungsroman

Its depiction of the assembly-line, of shopfloor racism, and its portrayal of the life of the immigrant and the role of women in the factories of heavy industry, are characteristics of *Elise* which naturally invite comparison with various proletarian writings, feminist exposés and/or the *témoignages* of, for example, francophone North African writers. Such thematic linkings are important; an investigation of them – an exploration of contemporaneous Algerian writings, or with more recent works by 'second generation' authors, or again with accounts such as those by Simone Weil – cannot but enrich understanding of many of the issues the novel raises. Thus surveys such as Ahsène Zehraoui's *Les Travailleurs algériens en France* (1976) testify to the accuracy of Etcherelli's portrayal of immigrant alienation in the '50s and '60s, and more recent works of fiction, or autobiographies such as Djura's *Le Voile du silence* (1990), [2] complement the novel by, for example, giving insights into the life during and after the Algerian war of a young Algerian girl in Paris.

But while *Elise,* by virtue of such issues, can, as demonstrated, be usefully contrasted with a surprisingly wide variety of works of fiction and non-fiction, this is also a novel rooted in a specifically literary tradition – namely, that of *Bildungsroman.* Goethe, Stendhal, Balzac, Dickens . . . the great names of the nineteenth century excelled in the *roman d'apprentissage* – and also, as she revealed in an interview, constituted Etcherelli's preferred reading matter. Of them all, Balzac in particular commanded her attention, a point worth bearing in mind during any consideration of the development of this novel. André Maurois has written of the young Rastignac that he is, in *Le Père Goriot,*

[2] Editions Michel Lafon.

'un personnage en devenir'. [3] And he continues: 'Il incarne le passage des illusions de l'adolescence aux dures expériences de l'homme'.

'Un personnage en devenir': the phrase sums up Eugène on his arrival in Paris, and is equally applicable to Elise in the same situation. In the early pages of the novel, which detail her life in the unnamed provincial town, no hint of 'becoming' is discernable in Elise; deprived of parents, colleagues (she works from home), or friends (offered up as sacrifices for Lucien), she defines herself by means of the maternal role adopted ostensibly for her brother's benefit, and in the name of which she fusses over him, follows him, and persuades herself of her superiority over other girls of her age. The carefully constructed isolation stunts character development, a fact underlined by the stress laid on the lack of physical development: Henri finds Elise, at 20, to be particularly small, and she herself comments that 'je paraissais très jeune' (p. 14/59).

If, however, there is a paucity of any stimuli likely to provoke Elise into expanding her horizons, the depicting of the effect of Lucien's post-convalescent *mal-de-vivre* on the household allows Etcherelli to reveal certain character traits which show there to be a strong personality behind the conservative dresser and the maternal prying. Lucien prefers silence first thing in the morning; his sister does not, and therefore tries constantly to impose her tastes: 'Parce qu'il me fallait une certaine atmosphère de sérénité, de gentillesse, je voulais l'obliger à y pénétrer" (p. 16/61). Far from being dominated or down-trodden, Elise, at this time the main wage-earner, is well-placed to goad her brother, and on occasion cannot resist doing so: 'toi, Lucien, tu fais ce que tu veux. Jusqu'à maintenant, il est vrai, tu as choisi de ne rien faire' (p. 17/62). It is Elise who arranges for Lucien to be interviewed for the *surveillant* post; when Lucien voices his displeasure at her meddling, she notes his resentment, but cannot forbear adding: 'Il y alla pourtant' (p. 18/63). In short, the self-effacing exterior and quiet ways conceal a decided, resourceful

[3] Preface to Balzac, *Le Père Goriot,* Livre de Poche, p. x.

young woman with a strong sense of irony – and a sensitivity which makes her particularly vulnerable to the rows that become commonplace in the cramped flat: 'me remontaient à la gorge des découragements, la sensation d'être envasée, et je restais quelques secondes la tête renversée, les yeux pleins de larmes' (p. 19/64).

Lucien's marriage, while it introduces another person into her restricted circle, paradoxically isolates Elise further; she will describe this as the unhappiest autumn of her life. Having read the odd article at Lucien's suggestion, to please him, Elise now begins reading all the books and magazines he brings home, in an effort to feel close to him. The younger brother behind whom she has for so long hidden now provides a key to the world around her; Elise's eyes are opened: 'Je me sentis vite concernée. Je vis ma condition, j'en devins fière' (p. 26/69).

From this point on Elise's circle of acquaintances expands (Marie is born, Henri reappears), and her understanding of others' lives does likewise (from despising her sister-in-law, Elise comes to value her gentle, uncomplaining nature). Her growing perceptiveness is brought out: she now notices the attraction that the 'odeur de pauvreté' (p. 30/73) holds for Henri, and can understand Marie-Louise's attempts to regain her husband's attention.

But when a routine rummage reveals Anna's letter, its revelations come as a great blow to Elise. Her brother's secret life, of which she cannot hope to be part, has been revealed thanks to a love-letter from a woman who evidently shares his political interests, and is attracted, and apparently attractive, to him. Given the obsessive nature of her love for her brother, it is this last point that is the most important. All mention of his having become sexually active has until now been avoided; it would seem that Elise has seen Marie-Louise, despite her evident sexual appeal, as a phase her brother must of necessity go through. (Of all the variations possible – *être enceinte, attendre un bébé, avoir un enfant* – Elise uses the most impersonal to refer to Marie-Louise's pregnancy: 'Je m'aperçus la première qu'il y aurait un enfant', p. 24/67.) She has been proved right; now, however, comes an unexpected threat she is unable to counter – the mutual attraction between her brother and an apparent soul-mate. Elise is in shock and in pain.

While a developing insight enables Elise to assess most accurately Lucien's life-strategy – '[il] s'était créé, pour survivre, des refuges imprenables: une certaine paresse, la quête de l'amour extraordinaire' (p. 40/81) – Etcherelli makes it clear that the intellectual development it points at is in advance of Elise's emotional maturing. Incensed at discovering that Lucien has borrowed from her to subsidise the hotel room he and Anna use, Elise orchestrates a confrontation about the household's finances. The scene is ugly and violent; it must, we feel, assuage the frustration Elise feels both at not being able to reveal her knowledge of the affair, and at the double standards she is acting by (reading her brother's mail was immoral, but done without misgivings; why then must she baulk at confronting him with her findings?). The family argument is the only outlet for her anger that she can permit herself.

The mere fact of Lucien and Anna's relationship stimulates Elise's sexual awareness. She begins immediately to notice Marie-Louise's attempts to increase her attractiveness to Lucien, and condemns these with the callousness of inexperience: 'Elle a lu dans un courrier du cœur imbécile qu'il fallait être plusieurs femmes en une. Mais les recettes pour accommoder un homme coûtent cher' (p. 42/83). When invited to meet Anna, she is both intrigued and alarmed; Etcherelli causes her to give the most detailed physical description in the novel of this her brother's lover, while having her stress that the conversation completely passes her by – she is too engrossed in trying both to see through Anna and her 'épais rimmel' (p. 49/89), and in trying to see her as her brother does. Anna has become 'competition'; registering the long straight hair, Elise instantly relates the observation back to herself: 'je me demande si cela m'irait de porter les miens libres' (p. 49/89).

Later, overhearing the two row, Elise loses all patience with them, and is filled with 'un brusque dégoût' (p. 54/93). Anna has claimed that she is pregnant; it is the implicit reference to sexual activity, which she invests with a sense of the territorial, that incenses Elise: 'Ils s'installaient partout. Quand ils avaient fait l'amour dans un lieu, ils y étaient chez eux'. Shortly after this argument, Lucien leaves for Paris. Elise has for the first time leisure for 'la contemplation de moi-même' (p. 58/96); she relaxes, reads, sleeps. But when news of her brother is slow in coming, the new-found independence crumbles, and the uncertainty, the strain, leaves Elise physically very vulnerable: 'Je crus plusieurs fois que ma vie allait partir dans les vertiges qui me terrassaient devant la boîte aux lettres vide' (p. 58/97).

Thus, when the invitation to join Lucien arrives, the sudden joy Elise feels at the idea of leaving is sublimated into a frenzy of activity in preparation of her departure: going to Paris is both a reaching out for a new life, and an escape from a situation – life without Lucien – that Elise is as yet unequal to.

By the time Elise joins Lucien, the reader has a very detailed picture of her life to date, of the genteel poverty, the cramped flat, the fruit boxes brought up to use as fuel, the nappies strung across the main room. Gaston de Zélicourt has observed how Balzac, in his role as social historian, 'accorde une importance extrême au milieu social et à ses incidences, jusqu'à faire de ce milieu le sujet principal d'œuvres capitales'. [4] Etcherelli his admirer is at pains both to depict her chosen milieu most vividly, *and* to provide contrasts to facilitate understanding; thus we are given glimpses into both the life led by Henri and his 'famille aisée sans histoires' (p. 30/73), and that of Anna in the room she shares with four others. If we are to follow the learning process Elise undergoes, and accurately evaluate the impact upon her of particular incidents, we need to know a considerable amount about her formative years.

No details are given about the first month Elise spends in Paris – but the arrival of Anna, which will occasion her second move in four weeks, ends her period of inactivity. She greets it with a searing condemnation of everything that is 'fabriqué', 'faux' (p. 69/104), calculated, and which Anna embodies. Elise is pitiless, but her very vehemence in turn earns her our pity;

[4] *Le Monde de la Comédie humaine,* Seghers, 1979, p. 15.

while 'être mêlée, un peu' (p. 71/106) in Lucien's life remains her chief objective, she will not easily progress to other relationships.

Starting work at the factory is the turning point for Elise. Never before has she been the focus of anyone's interest; her grandmother had been preoccupied with the troublesome grandchild, and then with his wife and child; Lucien, Marie-Louise and Anna have only ever been concerned with Lucien. Elise has been no-one's main concern; according to the definition in Anna's letter (to which she several times refers), she has never communicated fully – 'C'est, pendant quelques instants, exister et le savoir par un autre' (p. 37/79) – nor been communicated with. At the factory she is instantly attributed several different identities, and from the first, the attention pleases her: 'Je me sentais véritablement bien. [. . .] On s'occupait beaucoup de moi' (p. 73/108). She is Daubat's pupil, a sensible, conscientious worker he wants to protect; she quickly learns that flattery will keep her in his favour. She is the sister of the troublesome young Lucien; the French contingent have hopes that she will 'make him see sense'. She is a white Frenchwoman in a workshop populated mostly by immigrant workers who will presume she shares the outlook of Daubat and the *régleur.* Learning to assume these and other identities, she begins the process of defining which – who – she will choose to be.

Fear is the keynote of the first few days at the factory: fear of the anonymous huddle of wolf-whistling men, fear of being found wanting in her work; of not being strong enough. Against that background Etcherelli shows Elise obliged to abandon various long-held tenets (among these, the belief that one can never feel too tired to wash), and much of the old reticence. The interest in her own appearance and ability to attract attention that contact with Anna has inspired in her grows in this male-dominated working environment: the as yet unnamed Mustapha having pointed out that the other women do not wear their overalls as long as does Elise, it is stressed that, despite her tiredness, Elise spends one and a half hours shortening hers. That same evening, dining in her brother's room, she is again struck by

Anna's attractiveness, and obvious awareness of it; again is expressed the desire both to emulate her brother's lover, and to attract other men: 'Plairait-elle à Mustapha? Moi aussi j'avais les cheveux longs. J'aurais voulu que Mustapha le sût, ce petit singe malingre, méchant, qui m'avait demandé: "Pourquoi portez-vous votre blouse si longue?"' (p. 98/129). Subsequently she appears to regret what seems to her a provocative act – 'Mustapha sifflotait. J'avais craint qu'il ne remarquât ma blouse raccourcie et surtout mes cheveux' (p. 99/130) – but it is plain that what she fears is not that Mustapha should notice her amateurish attempts at self-improvement, but that he should attribute the effort to his own criticism.

For indeed Elise is now unconsciously preparing herself for a new relationship. Lucien and Anna's couple continues to occupy her thoughts – 'lui, il a Anna; entre la graisse et le cambouis [. . .] se glisse l'espérance faite amour, faite chair' (p. 98/130); as ever, its physicality is stressed. Elise's proud isolation has given way to a need of others: 'je me suis mise à aimer les êtres' (p. 99/130). And just as this admission is made, Arezki makes his appearance.

Barely minutes later, Elise is seized by a sudden thirst, described as 'ce désir brutal' (p. 100/131). Anne Ophir has suggested that this is a reaction to the fact that Mustapha and Arezki are talking about her in Arabic: 'Désir animal, seule réplique possible à la chosification menaçante. En devenant corps assoiffé Elise semble vouloir s'affirmer en tant qu'être vivant' (*15,* p. 193). A simpler explanation would be that the sudden, unavowed attraction has, as tradition would have any strong emotion do, caused Elise's throat to 'go dry'. Or again, given the figurative sense of the word 'thirst' in many languages, it may be that Elise's subconscious has identified something, *someone,* it thirsts to attain.

Heat, light, and the element containing both – fire – introduce Arezki's first appearance, and colour most subsequent descriptions of him. Passion, virility and power held in check are suggested when such images are, as often in francophone Algerian poetry, partially subdued to things dark, sombre: thus the 'feu noir allongé qui était son regard' (p. 100/131) hints, as does that image in Mostefa Lacheraf's 'Pays de longue peine', [5] at inner strength, and obsession. The effect upon Elise, originally experienced as thirst, spreads through her body; as she explains her symptoms, the nurse's first thought is of pregnancy. Elise is indignant; two pages on, a new 'nous' betrays the interest the newcomer already holds for her: 'Il travaillait vite et bien. Nous ne nous trouvâmes jamais ensemble' (p. 105/135).

The new experiences that life in Paris and at the factory are offering Elise are added to by the anti-war meeting that underlines her political naïvety; by the effect upon her of her continued reading; by the visit of the time-and-motion-studies man. But the slowly growing friendship with Arezki begins to dominate the narrative; furtive looks, timid smiles, and an obvious relief at Arezki's indifference to the new female arrivals punctuate a deft portrayal of burgeoning romance.

Elise's first outing with Arezki alerts her to the attention their mixed-race couple draws: she is at the end of the evening glad not to have been seen by colleagues. The next tableau sees her passively listening to Lucien describe to Henri the working conditions she now shares, and to Henri maintaining that the French workers' indifference to the war stems solely from ignorance. Neither man has, of course, like Elise, experienced the prejudice of which they speak 'at first hand'.

Subsequent outings see a sharpening both of Elise's sensual awareness, and her understanding of the complexities of the war, and the life of the 'enemy-immigrants'. She witnesses the intimidating police identity-check, a confused affair of police vans, guns, uniforms; the next day, the cloakroom conversation reveals the women's disdain for, indiscriminately, both the North African and the black workers. Elise's new-found awareness of her body, which aches each time Arezki lets the chance for a brief conver-

[5] 'Mais l'enfant-pâtre est loin sur les crêtes souveraines
Un feu vengeur s'allume entre ses mains
Un feu noir qui résonne au milieu des bourreaux.'
'Pays de longue peine', quoted in *Anthologie de la littérature algérienne*, Livre de Poche, 1990, p. 60.

sation slip by, reveals itself in her appreciation of the temptation that Didi, 'telle une appétissante sucrerie' (p. 151/175), must represent for the lonely workers.

However, despite her anguish when Arezki appears for a few days to ignore her, despite the developing solidarity she feels for him and his countrymen, Elise hesitates when he suggests she use with him the *tutoiement* she has to date employed with no man other than Lucien. Arezki's reaction to her reasons – that she has talked so much about Lucien that 'Je me suis demandé si tu étais vraiment sa sœur' (p. 158/181) – and the fact that he goes on to discuss a past love affair, underlines the ambiguous nature of the brother/sister relationship. Elise is in effect caught between two worlds; her hesitation, and the courage it will take to make a commitment to Arezki and to his world, are part of the process of self-definition that cannot be hurried.

It is important that Elise should be shown to be able to place her own experience in a wider context, the factory environment becoming with time claustrophobic. On one occasion Etcherelli shows her protagonist strolling through the cold winter streets around the Porte d'Italie, her observation of passers-by and of the attitudes and reactions she attributes to them constituting a form of *mise au point* of her experience to date. During a subsequent outing with Arezki she is able to summarise the thoughts of those watching their couple. No naïvety now remains; the matter-of-fact tone used to convey these insights paradoxically emphasises their intrinsic horror. (That same evening, Arezki's tentative suggestion that they may be able to see each other more often delights Elise – and proves to be the occasion for the writer to sound a personal note of thanks: this moment of pure happiness is spent in contemplation of . . . Falguière's statue of Balzac.)

Learning about herself and her own emotions through her relationship with Arezki, Elise is simultaneously made aware of the confusion the newly-arrived immigrant experiences, and subsequently, once Lucien and Mustapha have ensured the secret relationship is common knowledge, of their living conditions, their fears, their hopes. She glimpses the life of the pathetic, FLN-fearing uncle, and that of Arezki's friends in Nanterre; at the same time she shares in that immigrant experience as Bernier, aware of the relationship, makes no secret of his disapproval. Even Mustapha's friendship is withdrawn; loyalties are a complicated issue.

So too is love. Just before the police raid on Barbès interrupts what is to be her first sexual encounter, Elise automatically conjures up images of Lucien and Anna. It is as if she wants that relationship to act as a barometer for her own, while simultaneously recognising it as essentially very different from the one she and Arezki share:

> l'amour signifiait pour l'un ceci, pour l'autre le contraire, comment savoir et trancher? Celui d'Anna et de Lucien, je le percevais comme un long cri prolongé, une violente ruade où ils s'exterminaient et renaissaient, un jeu fou qui les isolait, les condamnait à la solitude, un navire errant qui n'accostait nulle part. (p. 221/234)

With the gradual emotional awakening in Elise comes a developing understanding of her new world and those peopling it. Mustapha spontaneous concert provides the occasion for Elise, who watches the watchers, to read their reactions. Lucien's illness sees her putting probing questions to the foreman Gilles, and holding her own most assertively as they talk. Lest we should, however, feel that too abrupt a change has taken place within her protagonist, Etcherelli has her occasionally produce a reflex worthy of her grandmother – as when she sees Anna while paying Lucien a visit in hospital: 'sale, sale fille, c'est elle qui l'a contaminé. Elle porte le mal . . .' (p. 243/253). And of course Elise can triumphantly reclaim the room Anna's initial arrival in Paris deprived her of – her behaviour in it is still, however, shaped by her awareness that Lucien and Anna have shared it: 'je me couchai comme j'avais vu Anna se coucher, et je défis mes cheveux pour lui ressembler' (p. 245/255).

Throughout the relationship with Arezki, a certain duplicity on Elise's part is underlined. Despite Arezki's plans to find a room, despite wanting one herself, Elise never speaks of the matter to anyone who might help. Despite Arezki's plans of moving to Bordeaux, she never pursues the issue; knowing what her grandmother's reaction would be, she has no wish to hurt him. Nor does she want to destroy what is patently a very comforting dream. But the dream must, in its very desperation, disturb her; it is inconceivable that an experienced FLN militant should imagine that one of the age, views and background of Elise's grandmother should consider welcoming him into her home – unless, that is, his hold on reality has slipped. Towards the close of the book, Elise and Arezki both sense he is experiencing a certain lack, but his explanation – 'Il me manque l'imagination' (p. 251/259) – does not ring true (particularly as he goes on to fantasise about buying Elise a blue-green dressing-gown and taking her to the sea). What he lacks is perhaps the ability to control the dreams: the ability never entirely to drop his guard, or forget the present.

This is surely the lack common to Arezki, to Lucien, to Elise, that to which she refers in her closing lines: 'Quelle force nous a manqué? Où est la faille qui ne nous a pas permis de dominer ce qu'il est facile d'appeler le destin?' (p. 275/280). One confirmed and one presumed death, and one survivor clinging to the wreckage; such is the price paid for dreams. 'Une des grandes leçons de la Comédie humaine', Zélicourt has suggested, is that 'le naufrage attend les hommes qui méconnaissent les réalités de la vie'. [6] Etcherelli can be said to propound in this novel a similar view; and if her protagonist emerges bruised but still battling, and convincingly so, it is because the learning process she has undergone has been shown to have led the naïve, priggish youngster towards the sensitive realism of maturity.

[6] *Le Monde de la Comédie humaine,* Seghers, 1979, p. 284.

8

After 'la vraie vie'

REVIEWING her third novel *Un arbre voyageur,* for *Le Nouvel Observateur,* Henri Guillemin observed that Claire Etcherelli's heroines 'ne savent pas, ne peuvent pas séparer leur drame personnel du drame collectif' (*24*). An accurate appraisal, but also an observation that underlined the emergence of an 'Etcherelli heroine', a character inhabiting the 'univers doux-amer' (*22,* p. 57) which has, after three novels, emerged as that with which the authoress has come to be associated. Elise Letellier was the first; it is of interest briefly to examine her links, and those of the world she inhabits, with the subsequent works.

Etcherelli's world, then, is that of the city poor: the 'chambre meublée', factory or shop-assistant work, scrimping. But it is also that of this milieu's 'marginaux', its atypical members – atypical in that all are politically concerned or indeed 'engagés'. Etcherelli protagonists are incapable of remaining on the sidelines of their era's political issues, of ignoring causes they judge to be just, of standing by when confronted by what they see as injustices. As Elise (and Lucien, and Henri) espouse the Algerian struggle for independence, *A propos de Clémence*'s eponymous heroine helps out at La Campa refugee camp for mainly Spanish immigrants, and *Un arbre voyageur*'s Milie rejects the offer of security from one who, bewildered at the political climate of spring 1968, can only sum it up as 'un vent de folie'.

As background to the events of these works lies Paris, with its richer districts around which the characters frequently walk, its *quartiers populaires* which they inhabit, its immediate suburbs beyond St Denis and St Ouen; in each novel, the nineteenth and twentieth arrondissements are specifically spotlighted. In each novel, too, newspaper headlines and/or radio bulletins punctuate the narrative, to create another kind of background: in *Clémence,* Anna's radio gives out the news of the deaths during the anti-OAS demonstration at the Charonne underground station, and later headlines detail unrest in Madrid, trials, French loans to Spain; in *Un arbre voyageur,* Milie hunches over the radio as it announces De Gaulle's departure for an unknown destination, and as the novel ends, news comes through of the invasion of Czechoslovakia.

In all three novels, as mentioned earlier, the character of Anna appears, her 'recurrence' perhaps another wink in the direction of the creator of *La Comédie humaine.* Initially Lucien's lover, she appears as room-mate to Clémence and lastly as close friend to Milie, entrusted with the narration of the first part of *Un arbre voyageur.* The opening pages of *Clémence* see her some three years after the death of Lucien ('un garçon mort bêtement sur une route', *1,* p. 31), 'recroquevillée dans l'impuissance, lovée dans l'inutilité' (*1,* p. 44). When Clémence leaves to live with Villaderda, Anna has no further excuse for this willed stagnation, and must take action. By the end of the novel she is, while still 'laconique et reservée' (*1,* p. 223), different – renewed: 'Elle est vivante'. As *Un arbre voyageur* opens, Anna has become 'raisonnable, efficace et énergique' (*2,* p. 10), despite herself and in response to the needs of her lover Serge; later, a mother, and for the moment at least, happy in a new relationship, she impresses Milie with 'sa vigueur, sa sérénité, son aisance' (*2,* p. 231). Her confidence, and 'une volonté d'aller jusqu'aux limites d'elle-même' (*2,* p. 230), both awe and encourage her friend.

What then of those protagonists in whose lives Anna plays her various roles? In Clémence (a pseudonym in the novel for authoress Gabrielle Fardoux), there is much of Elise. A solitary child, brought up in near poverty in an unnamed town that is doubtless Bordeaux, she leaves home after her mother's death to find work in Paris. She is drawn to the refugees of La Campa; to those needier than herself, to those who have a cause. Like Elise, she needs to be needed; her relationship with the exiled Villaderda, the focal point of the novel, is thus, for as long as it lasts, particularly fulfilling, as Clémence not only becomes his lover, but helps build up the business (selling Spanish language courses) that he is starting off. When ultimately Villaderda's self-destructive lack of trust pushes him to strike Clémence, vandalise their room and in effect strangle the relationship, we are in no doubt that like Elise, Clémence, passive, self-effacing, 'dure/douce' (*1,* p. 138), will survive. An Etcherelli heroine, the second novel makes apparent, is of necessity both resilient and resourceful; she bends in order not to break.

'L'arbre est un élément stable de la nature' (*18*), Etcherelli remarked while explaining some of the reasons for the apparently paradoxical title given her third novel. The tree can symbolise strength, fertility, shelter, a linking of heaven and earth (and by extension of the spiritual and the physical, mind and body) . . . and certainly she whom we would take to be the tree of the title, the novel's protagonist Milie, has something of each characteristic. (Although, like her predecessors, she must periodically uproot herself, move on, 'couper ponts et amarres', *2,* p. 177; these women learn *while journeying.*) Milie is the mother of three children, the first two by Georges, a somewhat more sympathetic Lucien-figure who rejects fatherhood and leaves to travel, the third by Mercier, warehouse militant, 'un pur' (*2,* p. 160) who dies before seeing his son. She acts as focal point, flame, around which circle Anna, the alcoholic Breton poet Fanch, the unwanted son of an acquaintance, and finally the considerate, unimaginative Walter. Tired, frail, disorganised, passive, patient, she provides shelter and succour for the extended family dependent on her – and hope, a vague belief in a new day, in 'l'enfant de mai' (*2,* p. 333) and what the events of 1968 might pave the way for, never dies out. Like Elise and Gabrielle/Clémence before her, she has the ability to triumph over both poverty and despair, to shore up well-intentioned, likeable and even charismatic men who are lacking in what Dominique Autrand has summed up as 'les réserves de vitalité, de combativité que toute femme possède' (*21,* p. 6).

Such, then, are Etcherelli's heroines, and such their milieu, a milieu which is indeed, as Simone de Beauvoir had it, 'difficile, ingrat mais non désespérant' (*22,* p. 58). It is a world conveyed by, amongst other things, multiple images associated with water in its various forms. Lucien dreams of a boat that will never drop anchor, Elise takes over that self-same dream; Clémence sees

Villaderda's business venture as their raft; Mercier's wife is compared to a boat in troubled waters, and Walter explains thus his incomprehension of Milie's reaction to the events of May: 'Tu fiches à l'eau toutes les bouées. Et après tu fais tanguer le bateau' (*2,* p. 313). Lives flow, boats are rocked, moorings are lost . . . and often throughout it all a fine rain falls. And against that background, 'des laissés pour compte' (*21,* p. 5), whose lives Etcherelli excels at rendering in that spare, precise and restrained prose, work towards, and persist in believing in, 'la vraie vie'.

Selective Bibliography

Books in French are published in Paris and those in English in London unless otherwise stated.

Dates in brackets refer to first publication.

I. OTHER WORKS BY CLAIRE ETCHERELLI

1. *A propos de Clémence,* Denoël, Collection Les Lettres Nouvelles, 1971.
2. *Un arbre voyageur,* Gallimard, 1978.

II. CRITICAL MATERIAL SPECIFICALLY ON *ELISE*

a) Interviews

3. Simone de Beauvoir, 'Ecoutez cette femme…', *Le Nouvel Observateur,* 156 (15-21 novembre 1967), 26-28.
4. Jean Gaugeard, 'Enfin Claire Etcherelli', *Les Lettres françaises,* 1210 (29 novembre-5 décembre 1967), 9.
5. Francine Mallet, 'Claire Etcherelli parle', *Le Monde [des Livres],* 7116 (29 novembre 1967), III.

b) Articles and chapters

6. Anon, 'Catching up', *The Times Literary Supplement,* 3472 (12 September 1968), 976.
7. Dominique Aury, 'Elise ou la vraie vie', *La Nouvelle Revue Française,* XVI, 181 (1 janvier 1968), 144-45.
8. Simone de Beauvoir, *Tout compte fait,* Gallimard (1972), pp. 64-67.
9. Charles Camproux, 'La langue et le style des écrivains: Claire Etcherelli; Elise ou la vraie vie', *Les Lettres françaises,* 1244 (7 août 1968), 14-15.
10. André Dalmas, 'Premiers romans', *Le Monde [des Livres],* 7068 (4 octobre 1967), II.
11. Nicole Fouletier-Smith, 'Les Nord-Africains en France: réalités et représentations littéraires', *The French Review,* LI, 5 (April 1978), 683-91.
12. Jean Gaugeard, 'Elise ou l'authenticité', *Les Lettres françaises,* 1203 (11 octobre 1967), 12.

13. Stuart Hood, 'Members of Society', *The Listener,* vol. 83, 2138 (19 March 1970), 382-83.
14. Christian Melchior-Bonnet, 'Sorti des presses', *A la page,* 44 (2 février 1968), 318-19.
15. Anne Ophir, *Regards féminins,* Denoël-Gonthier (1976), pp. 153-235.
16. John Roach, Introduction to *Elise ou la vraie vie,* Methuen, Twentieth Century Texts series (1985), reprinted Routledge (1989), pp. 1-52.

III. Critical material on other works by Claire Etcherelli

a) Interviews

17. Anon, 'Tenez-vous un journal intime? (VII) Claire Etcherelli: les carnets de bord d'une voyageuse', *Le Monde [des Livres],* 11682 (20 août 1982), 12.
18. Anne Manceron, 'L'écriture comme arme en vue d'un combat', *La Quinzaine Littéraire,* 281 (16-30 juin 1978), 6.
19. Yvette Romi, 'Le problème no. 1, c'est le racisme', *Le Nouvel Observateur,* 317 (7-12 décembre 1970), 55. Interview with Michel Drach on his film version of *Elise.*

b) Articles

20. Bernard Alliot, 'La petite musique pour matins blêmes de Claire Etcherelli', *Le Monde [des Livres],* 10381 (16 juin 1978), 17. Review of *Un arbre voyageur.*
21. Dominique Autrand, 'Claire Etcherelli fidèle à elle-même', *La Quinzaine Littéraire,* 281 (16-30 juin 1978), 5-6. Review of *Un arbre voyageur.*
22. Simone de Beauvoir, 'Portrait d'un exilé', *Le Nouvel Observateur,* 344 (14 juin 1971), 57-58. Review of *A propos de Clémence.*
23. Jean-Louis Bory, 'Le pain et les roses', *Le Nouvel Observateur,* 317 (7 décembre 1970), 55. Review of Drach's film.
24. Henri Guillemin, 'Les braises ardentes de l'espérance', *Le Nouvel Observateur,* 712 (3 juillet 1978), 56. Review of *Un arbre voyageur.*

IV. Other writings relevant

a) To Chapters 1 and 2:

25. Ian H. Birchall, 'Imperialism and class: the French war in Algeria', in *Europe and its others, vol. II,* ed. F. Barker, University of Essex (1985), pp. 162-74.
26. Bernard Droz and Evelyne Lever, *Histoire de la guerre d'Algérie 1954-62,* Seuil, 1982.

27. Alec G. Hargreaves ed., *Immigration in post-war France,* Methuen, Twentieth Century Texts, 1987.
28. Guy Le Moigne, *L'Immigration en France,* Presses Universitaires de France (Que sais-je? no. 2341), 1986.
29. Chester W. Obuchowski, 'Algeria; the tortured conscience', *The French Review,* XLII, 1 (October 1968), 90-103.
30. J. Talbott, *The War without a Name: France in Algeria 1954-62,* Faber & Faber, 1981.
31. Madeleine Trébous, *Migration and Development: the case of Algeria,* Paris: Development Centre of the Organisation for Economic Co-operation and Development (OECD), 1970.
32. Ahsène Zehraoui, *Les Travailleurs algériens en France,* Librairie François Maspéro, 1976.

b) To Chapters 3 and 4:

33. Geneviève Bollème, *Le Peuple par écrit,* Seuil, 1986.
34. Jean Bron, *Histoire du mouvement ouvrier français, Tome III,* Editions ouvrières, 1974.
35. Philippe Gavi, *Les Ouvriers: enquête,* Mercure de France, 1970.
36. Léon Lemonnier, *Populisme,* La Renaissance du livre, 1931.
37. Dorothée Letessier, *Le Voyage à Paimpol,* Seuil, 1980.
38. Paul A. Loffler, *Chronique de la littérature prolétarienne française (1930-39),* Rodez: Editions Subervie, 1967.
39. Michel Ragon, *Histoire de la littérature prolétarienne en France,* Albin Michel, 1973.
40. ———, *Les Ecrivains du peuple,* Collection Germinal, 1947.
41. Roger Vailland, *325.000 francs,* Livre de Poche, 1990 (1955).
42. Simone Weil, *La Condition ouvrière,* Gallimard, 1979 (1951).

ADDENDUM

The reader's attention is also drawn to the following, published since the present work was submitted for publication:

43. Margaret Atack, 'The Politics of Identity in *Elise ou la vraie vie*', in *Contemporary French Fiction by Women,* ed. M. Atack and P. Powrie, Manchester University Press, 1990.
44. Sara Poole, 'Street-signs: The City as Context and as Code in the Novels of Claire Etcherelli', *Studies in Twentieth Century Literature,* vol. 18, no. 2, Summer 1994, pp. 189-201.

CRITICAL GUIDES TO FRENCH TEXTS

edited by

Roger Little, Wolfgang van Emden, David Williams

1. **David Bellos.** Balzac: La Cousine Bette.
2. **Rosemarie Jones.** Camus: L'Etranger *and* La Chute.
3. **W.D Redfern.** Queneau: Zazie dans le métro.
4. **R.C. Knight.** Corneille: Horace.
5. **Christopher Todd.** Voltaire: Dictionnaire philosophique.
6. **J.P. Little.** Beckett: En attendant Godot *and* Fin de partie.
7. **Donald Adamson.** Balzac: Illusions perdues.
8. **David Coward.** Duras: Moderato cantabile.
9. **Michael Tilby.** Gide: Les Faux-Monnayeurs.
10. **Vivienne Mylne.** Diderot: La Religieuse.
11. **Elizabeth Fallaize.** Malraux: La Voie Royale.
12. **H.T Barnwell.** Molière: Le Malade imaginaire.
13. **Graham E. Rodmell.** Marivaux: Le Jeu de l'amour et du hasard *and* Les Fausses Confidences.
14. **Keith Wren.** Hugo: Hernani *and* Ruy Blas.
15. **Peter S. Noble.** Beroul's Tristan *and the* Folie de Berne.
16. **Paula Clifford.** Marie de France: Lais.
17. **David Coward.** Marivaux: La Vie de Marianne *and* Le Paysan parvenu.
18. **J.H. Broome.** Molière: L'Ecole des femmes *and* Le Misanthrope.
19. **B.G. Garnham.** Robbe-Grillet: Les Gommes *and* Le Voyeur.
20. **J.P. Short.** Racine: Phèdre.
21. **Robert Niklaus.** Beaumarchais: Le Mariage de Figaro.
22. **Anthony Cheal Pugh.** Simon: Histoire.
23. **Lucie Polak.** Chrétien de Troyes: Cligés.
24. **John Cruickshank.** Pascal: Pensées.
25. **Ceri Crossley.** Musset: Lorenzaccio.
26. **J.W Scott.** Madame de Lafayette: La Princesse de Clèves.
27. **John Holyoake.** Montaigne: Essais.
28. **Peter Jimack.** Rousseau: Emile.
29. **Roger Little.** Rimbaud: Illuminations.

30. **Barbara Wright and David Scott.** Baudelaire: La Fanfarlo *and* Le Spleen de Paris.
31. **Haydn Mason.** Cyrano de Bergerac: L'Autre Monde.
32. **Glyn S. Burgess.** Chrétien de Troyes: Erec et Enide.
33. **S. Beynon John.** Anouilh: L'Alouette *and* Pauvre Bitos.
34. **Robin Buss.** Vigny: Chatterton.
35. **David Williams.** Rousseau: Les Rêveries du promeneur solitaire.
36. **Ronnie Butler.** Zola: La Terre.
37. **John Fox.** Villon: Poems.
38. **C.E.J. Dolamore.** Ionesco: Rhinocéros.
39. **Robert Lethbridge.** Maupassant: Pierre et Jean.
40. **David Curtis.** Descartes: Discours de la Méthode.
41. **Peter Cogman.** Hugo: Les Contemplations.
42. **Rosemary Lloyd.** Mallarmé: Poésies.
43. **M. Adereth.** Aragon: The Resistance Poems.
44. **Keith Wren.** Vigny: Les Destinées.
45. **Kathleen M. Hall and Margaret B. Wells.** Du Bellay: Poems.
46. **Geoffrey Bremner.** Diderot: Jacques le fataliste.
47. **Peter Dunwoodie.** Camus: L'Envers et l'Endroit *and* L'Exil et le Royaume.
48. **Michael Sheringham.** Beckett: Molloy.
49. **J.F. Falvey.** Diderot: Le Neveu de Rameau.
50. **Dennis Fletcher.** Voltaire: Lettres philosophiques.
51. **Philip Robinson.** Bernardin de Saint-Pierre: Paul et Virginie.
52. **Richard Griffiths.** Garnier: Les Juifves.
53. **Paula Clifford.** La Chastelaine de Vergi *and* Jean Renart: Le Lai de l'ombre.
54. **Robin Buss.** Cocteau: Les Enfants terribles.
55. **Tony Hunt.** Chrétien de Troyes: Yvain.
56. **Robert Gibson.** Alain-Fournier: Le Grand Meaulnes.
57. **James J. Supple.** Racine: Bérénice.
58. **Timothy Unwin.** Constant: Adolphe.
59. **David Shaw.** Molière: Les Précieuses ridicules.
60. **Roger Cardinal.** Breton: Nadja.

61. **Geoffrey N. Bromiley.** Thomas's Tristan *and the* Folie Tristan d'Oxford.
62. **R.J. Howells.** Rousseau: Julie ou la Nouvelle Héloïse.
63. **George Evans.** Lesage: Crispin rival de son maître *and* Turcaret.
64. **Paul Reed.** Sartre: La Nausée.
65. **Roger Mclure.** Sarraute: Le Planétarium.
66. **Denis Boak.** Sartre: Les Mots.
67. **Pamela M. Moores.** Vallès: L'Enfant.
68. **Simon Davies.** Laclos: Les Liaisons dangereuses.
69. **Keith Beaumont.** Jarry: Ubu Roi.
70. **G.J. Mallinson.** Molière: L'Avare.
71. **Susan Taylor-Horrex.** Verlaine: Fêtes galantes *and* Romances sans paroles.
72. **Malcolm Cook.** Lesage: Gil Blas.
73. **Sheila Bell.** Sarraute: Portrait d'un inconnu *and* Vous les entendez?
74. **W.D. Howarth.** Corneille: Le Cid.
75. **Peter Jimack.** Diderot: Supplément au Voyage de Bougainville.
76. **Christopher Lloyd.** Maupassant: Bel-Ami.
77. **David H. Walker.** Gide: Les Nourritures terrestres *and* La Symphonie pastorale
78. **Noël Peacock.** Molière: Les Femmes savantes.
79. **Jean H. Duffy.** Butor: La Modification.
80. **J.P. Little.** Genet: Les Nègres.
81. **John Campbell.** Racine: Britannicus.
82. **Malcolm Quainton.** D'Aubigné: Les Tragiques.
83. **Henry Phillips.** Racine: Mithridate.
84. **S. Beynon John.** Saint-Exupéry: Vol de Nuit *and* Terre des hommes.
85. **John Trethewey.** Corneille: L'Illusion comique *and* Le Menteur.
86. **John Dunkley.** Beaumarchais: Le Barbier de Séville.
87. **Valerie Minogue.** Zola: L'Assommoir.
88. **Kathleen Hall.** Rabelais: Pantagruel *and* Gargantua.

89. **A.W. Raitt.** Flaubert: Trois contes.
90. **Toby Garfitt.** Mauriac: Thérèse Desqueyroux.
91. **Margaret M. Callander.** Colette: Le Blé en herbe *and* La Chatte.
92. **David Whitton.** Molière: Le Bourgeois gentilhomme.
93. **Peter Cogman.** Mérimée: Colomba *and* Carmen.
94. **Derek A. Watts.** Corneille: Rodogune *and* Nicomède.
95. **Russell Cousins.** Zola: Thérèse Raquin.
96. **David Coward.** Pagnol: La Gloire de mon père *and* Le Château de ma mère.
97. **Kathleen M. McKilligan.** Mauriac: Le Nœud de vipères.
98. **Keith Busby.** Chrétien de Troyes: Perceval (Le Conte du Graal).
99. **Renate Günther.** Duras: Le Ravissement de Lol V. Stein *and* L'Amant.
100. **R.A. Francis.** Prévost: Manon Lescaut.